GAGA

GAGA

JOHNNY MORGAN

STERLING

New York / London
www.sterlingpublishing.com

Acknowledgement
To Laura Fragnito for her inspiration.

STERLING and the distinctive Sterling logo are registered
trademarks of Sterling Publishing Co., Inc.

10   9   8   7   6   5   4   3   2   1

Published by Sterling Publishing Co., Inc.
387 Park Avenue South, New York, NY 10016

This publication has not been prepared, approved, or licensed by the artist
Lady Gaga, her management, or any affiliated entities or corporations.

Distributed in Canada by Sterling Publishing
c/o Canadian Manda Group, 165 Dufferin Street
Toronto, Ontario, Canada M6K 3H6
Distributed in the United Kingdom by GMC Distribution Services
Castle Place, 166 High Street, Lewes, East Sussex, England BN7 1XU
Distributed in Australia by Capricorn Link (Australia) Pty. Ltd.
P.O. Box 704, Windsor, NSW 2756, Australia

Produced for Sterling Publishing by Essential Works
www.essentialworks.co.uk

Publishing Director: Mal Peachey
Managing Director: John Conway
Editors: Jennifer Eiss, Miranda Harrison, Fiona Screen
Designer: Michael Gray

Printed in China

Sterling ISBN 978-1-4027-8059-2

For information about custom editions, special sales, premium and
corporate purchases, please contact Sterling Special Sales Department
at 800-805-5489 or specialsales@sterlingpublishing.com

Contents

ALL WE HEAR IS LADY GAGA . . .

First they called her Stef.

Then they called her "The Germ."

But now they call her "LADY GAGA."

In an age of wannabe Britneys, interchangeable Pussycat Dolls, and made-by-TV pop stars, she dares to be DIFFERENT.

She used to be Stefani Joanne Angelina Germanotta, born March 1986, resident of the Upper West side of Manhattan, New York, New York, and problem pupil of the Convent of the Sacred Heart (1997–2002).

At school she was teased and laughed at by photofit, posh Upper East side princesses who claimed that she was never seen with her midriff covered, and that she and Britney Spears had been separated at birth.

Now it's Britney who wishes that.

Stef was always singing, dancing, acting. She came from the wrong side of town and she didn't care who knew, because she loved her mom Cynthia, dad Joe, and sister Natali, too.

At home, at friends' homes, and in public, at age 13, 14, 15, she played her dad's music—Springsteen, Joel, Bowie, Elton—and sang along out loud. She also sang along with Britney, Madonna, and Mary J. Blige, or her Mom's faves Cyndi Lauper, Boy George, and Grace Jones.

At age 16 Cynthia took Stef to NYC niteclubs and watched, smiling, as her daughter played piano and sang her heart out, her hands gesturing, waving, conducting, punching the air and the keys as she played.

Now she has a different sound, a different name, and a wholly new, different look—every time that she goes out in public.

She's now the BIGGEST POP STAR in the whole wide world and has redefined the meaning of FAME.

She is LADY GAGA and this is her story.

1

STEF

The Lady Gaga that we see today is ever-evolving, each move is choreographed to the sound of a pop-art-fashion soundtrack. Her rise to world-superstardom has been incessant, rapid, and all-conquering. Until she came along it had been assumed by many people in the music business (and beyond) that global music superstars were a thing of the past, that nostalgia ruled the airwaves and filled the concert halls. Lady Gaga has changed that idea.

Lady Gaga is a walking, talking, singing, performing composite of classic, new, and spontaneous combustions that power her every utterance and move. Those combustions were created in the greatest city on earth, the naked city of eight million stories, the city that never sleeps, the city so good they named it twice: New York, New York.

Gaga may now reside in a different world, one where the word "FAME" is stamped on the front of its passport, but she was made in NYC. In the years when her parents were growing up New York was a dangerous, frightening, exhilarating, and astounding place. In the 1960s and '70s wave after wave of avant-garde artists, musicians, and fashionistas developed their own New York state of mind and put that into their work. The Germanottas were lucky enough to see and hear first-hand the emerging musical talents of Bruce Springsteen, Billy Joel, Laura Nyro, Blondie, the Ramones, and Talking Heads, as they emerged from clubs and bars where their audiences dressed and acted differently to anywhere else in the world. New York was a unique experience, where high society rubbed fur coats with paint-splattered, ripped, and torn punk designers. New ideas, new business, new art, new music, and New York were synonymous. By the time that Joe and Cynthia started making babies they were beginning to make it there . . .

Opposite: Gaga makes an entrance on to the world stage, promoting "Just Dance" in Sydney, Australia, 2008.

SO GOOD . . .

I N the middle of the 1980s New York was at the epicenter of a "greed is good" economic boom, which had given birth to a new generation of materialistic high-earning professionals who were called "Yuppies" (Young Urban Professionals). After a term of Ronald Reagan–led government had turned around an economic depression, earning him a second term in office, America had moved smoothly into a new financially successful era. Money flowed through the city from the financial district to Village artists' lofts, uptown to designer stores, and out to the Hamptons where New Yorkers who had really "made it" spent their summers, or at least the whole of August.

Hollywood was busy making movies that mythologized and promoted the idea of New York as the center of the world, whether your world was built on dreams of money (Oliver Stone's *Wall Street* of 1987), escape (*Desperately Seeking Susan* starring Madonna, 1985), artistic paranoia (Martin Scorsese's *After Hours*, 1985), or supernatural laughs (*Ghostbusters*, 1984). The streets of New York were a perfect, ready-built movie set. The skyscrapers, Central Park, Fifth Avenue, and Village lofts were visual statements of an attitude that was pure New York. As the song says, if you can make it there, you can make it anywhere.

By 1985 Joe and Cynthia Germanotta were making their way in the emerging field of computer communications and were ready to make a family. By the time that their first child was born, Cynthia, who'd grown up in the Midwest,

Below: The Pythian building on West 70th Street, between Columbus and Broadway, has been the Germanotta family home since 1993.

was thirty-two years old, while New York native Joe was almost thirty.

Stefani Joanne was born on March 28, 1986, just as Madonna's "Live to Tell" single and video were released; looking back it's almost as if, sensing something was in the air, Madonna opted to debut a whole new look for that release. She appeared for the first time in public without what had become her trademark jewelry and underwear on show, opting instead for a 1930s-style dress and understated makeup.

In 1991 Stefani's baby sister Natali was born and the two Germanotta girls grew up as close friends and confidantes, it seems. Stefani showed an early love for music, which was encouraged by Poppa Joe, who had wanted to be a professional musician before discovering that his real talent lay in the emerging digital communications business. Joe and Cynthia created a company together that developed ways to make computers talk to each other. In the process discovered how a thing called "the internet" was going to revolutionize the world. They made some smart business choices, investing what little they had in new technology companies springing up that were progressing telecommunications, networking, and digital processing. Their hunches paid off as the new decade dawned and the rest of the world began to switch from faxes, telegrams, and typewriters to personal computers, which could do all of that but faster, cheaper, and more efficiently.

In 1993, flush with success, the Germanottas took on a $370,000 mortgage and moved into

a classy condominium building on the Upper West side of Manhattan. Situated on West 70th Street between Columbus and Broadway, the 1927-built Pythian, with its ornate blue and gold Egyptian façade, could almost have been plucked from a Parisian arrondissement and set down in New York. It was originally built as a meeting place and auditorium for a secret society called the Order of the Knights of Pythias, and the exterior had very few windows—the architect who designed it, Thomas Lamb, was famous for his 1920s' cinema palaces. The building was converted into eighty-four apartments over its eleven stories in 1984, but sympathetically so, keeping as many of the ornate features of the original as possible. Every apartment is unique and they remain highly sought-after. In 2010 a two-bedroom and two-bathroom apartment cost $2 million, with four-bedroom apartments fetching $3.25 million while a one-bedroom apartment cost $7,000 a month to rent.

Stefani grew up in a New York palace, was loved like a princess, and had an enchanted childhood.

> "My parents were very supportive of anything creative I wanted to do, whether it was playing piano or being in plays or taking method acting classes, which I did when I was eleven. They liked that I was a motivated young person."

CROSSTOWN TRAFFIC

LIFE on the Upper West side might have been dream-like in some ways, but the realities of a young girl's day are similar wherever you grow up. Everyone has to go to school. Of course, not every girl goes to a Disney-like castle of a convent, but that's where Stefani was sent. There had been talk among the family of her attending the Juilliard, a specialist, highly successful, and well-known music academy situated ten blocks south of the Pythian, but despite picking out notes on a piano since the age of four, Stefani wasn't always as diligent at practicing as students at the Juilliard are expected to be. And so instead, from the age of eleven she made a daily trek across Central Park to the Upper East side and the Convent of the Sacred Heart school on the corner of East 91st Street and Fifth Avenue. Just two blocks north of Frank Lloyd Wright's Guggenheim Museum, the Convent is situated in a quiet and hugely affluent neighborhood. Residents of the Upper East side look down on those of the Upper West side and consider themselves the truly wealthy of Manhattan.

The daughters of "old" money, the kind of families who claim a link to the founding fathers or at least the great industrialists of the nineteenth century, are the usual attendees of the Sacred Heart. Indeed, two years ahead of Stefani, Paris Hilton was probably the most rebellious pupil the Sisters had encountered. Until Stefani began to find her feet there, that is.

Stefani seems to have made many friends at Sacred Heart, and like her they shared a love of drama, dance, and performance. The Convent encouraged the study of music, although it was mainly classical in style. But by her second year at the Sacred Heart, Stef, as her friends had taken to calling her, was sharing some distinctly non-classical music with them. At the beginning

Left: Stef and her Sacred Heart Senior Class group in 2004 (the year that she graduated).

of 1999 a new pop star entered the charts and created a sensation: Britney Spears was only five years older than Stef and her friends, and they could all see some of themselves in her.

In the previous two years the biggest selling female act in America had been Cher. Her outfits, videos, and music were fun, but she was so old. Even Madonna was kind of old; there hadn't been a young female star who was so like Stef and her gang before, ever. Later that year Christina Aguilera released her first album and together she and Britney began to seriously challenge the rule of boy bands in the charts. The popularity of Backstreet Boys and Boyz II Men was starting to wane in the face of competition from the girls, plus a new boy band named 'N Sync. There was also Eminem, whose *Slim Shady LP* came out in February 1999, and a new, smooth rapper named Puff Daddy, whose debut album came out in August 1999.

"I was always very different and trying not to fit in too much. I got really good grades—I was like a straight-A student— but I was really bad. I was very naughty, wore awful things to school. I used to roll my skirt up really high so the nuns didn't know what to do with me."

Pop music was changing. It was becoming dangerous, cool, and seriously sexy—or at least concerned with sex. The accompanying video for it would more often than not contain images that were sexually knowing, or reveal lots of bare flesh, particularly in the midriff area. That was something Stef had noticed, and she copied it.

Living in Manhattan gave Sacred Heart girls a kind of access to some of the new pop stars, since MTV and the major network broadcasters had studios in central Manhattan where acts would record live performances.

Above: Stefani's school, the Convent of the Sacred Heart, on the corner of East 91st Street and Fifth Avenue.

"You really don't need to be a celebrity or have money or have the paparazzi following you around to be famous. Me and my friends just simply declared fame on our own, and we made art, and we said, 'This is the future' and we dressed in a way that said, 'This is fashion.'"

CULTURE CLUB

SEEING the success that Britney enjoyed inspired the young Stef to write some songs of her own. Seated at the piano on which she had learned to play classical pieces, Stef was able to pick out melodies that reflected the songs she was listening to. Being her Daddy's girl, she had always listened to the music Joe grew up with and played around the apartment. As she would later explain to *Rolling Stone* magazine, "My dad's a Jersey-born Italian, so I grew up listening to Springsteen albums that still had sand on them from the Shore. When I was a freshman in high school, I was in a cover band that did Zeppelin and Floyd and Jefferson Airplane—that was his brainwashing coming to fruition."

Her mom introduced Stef to some different kinds of pop music of the 1980s, among which were records by a British band called Culture Club. Their frontman, Boy George, was an androgynous-seeming character who sang in a camp falsetto voice. George wore Kabuki-style white pan makeup, a large hat, lots of jewelry, and over-sized baggy coats and pants (which often hid his growing bulk). The band's biggest hit, "Karma Chameleon," spent three weeks at Number 1 in the U.S.A. in 1984 and inspired waves of arty kids who felt that they were "different" to express themselves in a way that previously only Cyndi Lauper (see page 38)—another of Stef's mother's faves—had done.

With MTV playing all kinds of different music, twenty-four hours a day, and living in a densely populated metropolis where music blared from open windows on hot days—to say nothing of the music played in every store on Fifth Avenue—it was impossible for an impressionable, music- and performance-obsessed teenager not to be inspired by all kinds of different music. Even Judy Garland has had a namecheck from Lady Gaga.

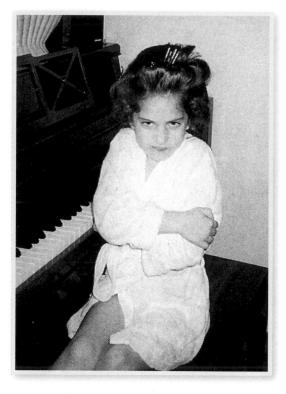

Previous page: Gaga wows Paris, September 2009.

Left: Stef showing determined spirit at the piano in 1995.

Still, Stef performed while seated at a piano and sang songs that were written at the piano and were often ballads. The overriding influences that the fifteen-year-old showed when performing were more in the vein of her dad's faves than anyone else. There are traces of Springsteen, Billy Joel, Elton John, and perhaps Carole King with a bit of Laura Nyro, thrown into the mix of her very early songs.

The piano was the place where she clearly felt most at home, though, and when she became the international phenomenon that is Lady Gaga, the fact that she could really play the instrument surprised people, particularly among the cynical Press corps. Her obvious musicianship has earned Gaga much respect from music fans who might, at first glance, assume that the singer in the weird get-up was nothing more than a mannequin, a blonde lip-syncing

"Bach and most of the classical stuff that I played when I was younger—the chord progression is the same as in pop music. It's ingrained in your sensibility about structure and discipline."

model who was paid by the hour simply to sing someone else's songs.

As we know though, Gaga writes all of her own material and thinks about how to surprise people with them musically, as well as visually. After earning a reputation as a pop star who performs songs with a dance feel to them, it must have surprised some people when they heard a song like "Brown Eyes," with its rock ballad feel. In many ways that song is a product of her very early listening habits.

Not that Gaga is likely to be put in any particular box and easily filed away. As she said in an interview in 2009, "I actually wouldn't consider myself a dance artist. I think I'm bridging the gap in a few different ways, and it's mostly from a music conceptual standpoint, mixing retro dance beats with more urban melodies, and a certainly pop chorus. It's really about, in a very methodic way, almost choosing exactly what pieces of what I want to have in the record, and then watching it cross over, with my fingers crossed." Cross-over is probably the right phrase here, and the more success Gaga gets, the more people succumb to her charms, then the more radical and inventive she could become.

Below: A bubbly performance at the Grammy Celebration Tour, Boston, May 2009.

PAPA DON'T PREACH

For all of Lady Gaga's uncompromising performances and irreverent statements, she did not—until the "Alejandro" video—mess with any overtly religious iconography. She didn't appear on stage "crucified" or use a crucifix as a sex toy. None of the images used on the covers of her albums or singles have referenced any directly religious symbolism. Admittedly there are rosary beads on display in the "Alejandro" video (when she wore a rubber nun costume), but her lyrics have not made any religious references either in support of, or against, Catholic doctrine. The shock of seeing Gaga dressed as a nun in the "Alejandro" video was perhaps greater because of that.

As shocking as Lady Gaga has been, is, and will be in the future, there's perhaps little chance of her ever overly using Christianity as a tool to sell product again. And that is partly because of her schooling, but mostly because she loves her parents and she is a good Catholic. Sacred Heart may have had a religiously informed curriculum, strict dress and behavior codes, and insisted on students doing anywhere between two and four hours of homework each night, but Stef didn't hate it there. Not at all.

Looking at photographs of the event it seems that Stefani was proud to take her confirmation and loved the floaty dress and tiara she wore for it. Her years at Sacred Heart allowed Stef to rebel within reason. The strict rules of the Convent were easily and quite tamely flaunted—raising the hem of her skirt above the knee, tying her blouse in a knot in order to show off her navel just like Britney, wearing lipstick; all "shocking" behavior that must have annoyed or even worried the sisters who taught at Sacred Heart. But there were no crack or dope dealers hanging around the school gates selling wraps to the girls. Instead there were lines of limos outside waiting for students. Like any school, of course, cliques formed, and some girls who had more of everything than anyone else would only hang with girls who had nearly as much, excluding the "weird" kids like Stef who, while not exactly poor, certainly wasn't the heir to a hotel fortune (unlike the Hilton sisters). Not that Stef knew the now infamous Paris, as she explained. "I never saw Paris, she was older than me, and it's funny that the press always write that I went to school with the Hilton sisters, but I actually only went with Nicky. Paris, I believe, left and went to Dwight."

Stef had enough friends at Sacred Heart to have only good memories of the place. Her parents worked hard to get her the kind of exclusive education that so few girls get a chance to enjoy. She knew that being, she said, "from a different social class from the other girls" made her different, and she played up that difference. It made some people like her. "I dressed differently," she recalled, "but I was focused, determined. I didn't really fit in, but I had friends because I'm a nice girl . . . and fun to party with!"

The parties with the Sacred Heart girls were innocent occasions, largely. It would be a couple of years after leaving the Convent before Stef's partying got close to disappointing and upsetting her dad.

"I was always a weird girl in school, who did theater and came to school with lots of red lipstick on or my hair perfectly curled, or whatever I was doing to get attention."

GAGA GODDESS
MADONNA

"I don't wanna be the next Madonna. I want to be the next Lady Gaga but I'm really very flattered by the comparison. I really admire her as a female performer."

BLONDE AMBITION

She came out of the arty, Lower East side gay dance scene, a pop star who'd paid her dues singing in bars and clubs—an Italian-American blonde full of ambition and attitude, with lots of ideas about fashion, art, and music that had been formed while completing only a year at performance college. Madonna Ciccone's early career reads like a blueprint for that of Lady Gaga, and comparisons between the women have been constantly made in the press. Madonna, who was born in 1958, is old enough to be Gaga's mother, even if she continued to perform energetic live shows full of spectacle and explosions into the fourth decade of her career.

The press have made countless lazy comparisons between Ms. Ciccone and Ms. Germanotta, and they have not all been about the color of their hair or provocative dress sense. There's a vague idea among journalists too young to have first-hand memories of the era that, when Madonna broke into the pop limelight, she made as big a splash as Lady Gaga has done. In fact, however, it wasn't until the release of her sophomore album, *Like a Virgin*, that Madonna became an international star. Her self-titled debut album took almost a year to climb the charts, while her first single, "Everybody," failed to chart at all. Neither did the second single taken from it: "Burning Up." However, the third Madonna single, "Holiday," became a big success and helped push the album into the charts around the world. Madonna's next single, "Lucky Star," became her first Top Five hit and the video that accompanied it showed off the Madonna look, which soon became the rage around the world: lots of jewelry, mesh fingerless gloves, bare midriff, leggings, and messy hair with a huge bow in it. The video wasn't exactly expensive to make—there's just her and two male dancers on a white background—and neither was it shocking. Madonna spent the whole of her first couple of years as a professional singer promoting her debut album by miming in clubs in New York, London, and Los Angeles, and by appearing on as many music television shows as possible in order to get her name and face known. It wasn't until she was ready to promote her second album that Madonna put together a "real" tour with a band, dancers, and special effects. The Virgin Tour of 1985 was panned by music critics—and loved by fans.

The single of "Like a Virgin" was an international hit, propelled by heavy rotational play of the video on MTV. Today that video looks faintly ridiculous. In it Madonna dances and mimes on a gondola as it journeys through Venice, a scene intercut with Madonna miming while wearing a short, white wedding dress inside a Venetian palace that has a lion (a real, live lion) patrolling its terraces. As the video ends we see Madonna being carried to an ornate bed by a man whose face, we finally discover, is that of a lion. Except it looks like a lion mask you'd buy at a joke store. However, in 1985, the video was considered a bit of a masterpiece. The song must take all of the credit, though. The mix of overtly sexual lyrics and synthesizer-produced disco beat with its catchy chorus had people singing along from their first hearing.

While, like Gaga, Madonna had begun her career living in the New York artist district, once she'd made it as a solo star Ms. Ciccone mixed only with Hollywood and fashion royalty. She moved into making movies as soon as she was asked, married a movie star (Sean Penn), made friends with fashion designers Jean Paul Gaultier and Gianni Versace, and used the fashion magazine *Vogue* as inspiration for another of her biggest hits. Madonna's fashion statements were pretty tame, though. Gaga's are wholly original and cutting-edge. Comparisons between the pair are superficial and immaterial.

Opposite: Lady Gaga and Madonna at the Marc Jacobs fashion show, New York Fashion Week, September 2009.

CAPTIVATED

By the turn of the 21st century, it seemed that Madonna's career was almost over. Reduced to covering songs from the early 1970s (Don McLean's "American Pie") and "starring" in increasingly poor movies, she had been eclipsed by Britney as *the* female pop star of the day and was almost eclipsed by the careers of Christina Aguilera and Missy Elliott, too. In fact, it would take an appearance with all three at the 2003 MTV Music Video Awards show to put her back into the spotlight. A new generation of fans may or may not have been won over by her smooching with both Britney and Christina on the TV.

Whether the infamous "kiss" had an effect on Stefani Germanotta is debatable. She was far too busy preparing herself for her just beginning career as a singer-songwriter in New York.

At age sixteen Stefani had begun to sing and play in front of live audiences in her hometown. She also attended auditions for parts in shows in the city, though with little success. She did appear in school and student plays, where she was renowned for getting so totally and truly into character for each play that she'd refuse to answer to any but the characters' names, even when not onstage. Stef's immersion in the stage was so all-consuming as her time at the Sacred Heart came to an end, that she was encouraged by her mother to apply to New York University to study drama and performance—specifically the Collaborative Arts Project 21, which is a faculty of the Tisch School of The Arts.

Stef attended CAP21, as it's known, at their Conservatory building on West 18th Street where she began a course of learning on how to perform (act, sing, and dance) for musical theater. A relatively new faculty—it was established in 1993—it began, according to its own literature, "in response to the need for in-depth actor training for the musical theater." Since 1995 CAP21 has produced students who have gone on to perform in countless hit Broadway musicals—among them several that Stef would probably love to have been in, such as *Wicked*, *Cabaret*, and *Legally Blonde*.

However, the first year of the course that Stef undertook was spent learning about the business, writing essays, and reading text books. Her first term at college was not just about performing, though there was also plenty of that, too. Some students undoubtedly found the written part of the course work a drag, though Stef would later (when she became Gaga) state that she loved writing essays and reading text books while studying in her first and only year there.

Being part of such a prestigious performance course could and did naturally bring students to the attention of TV, film, and theater professionals. Tisch students often got the chance to play extras or play bit parts in different media.

Stef tried for and passed auditions while at CAP21. During her time there she played the part of an unsuspecting customer in a diner where MTV's *Boiling Point: 14* was being filmed. For the show "customers" are "secretly" filmed ordering a meal—they must be alone in the diner—and receiving a call on the cell. They are asked by a manager to leave the diner while they talk. On returning the customer finds their meal is missing; they ask for it back and the "waitress" brings it to their table laden with junk—cellophane wrap, discarded napkins, and so on. The "waitress" then has to get the customer to explode with anger within fourteen minutes, or else the "customer" has won. Films of three "customers" are intercut with each other. Stef is filmed along with a similar-aged girl and guy who take the terrible service that they get in a much calmer way than she does, as she finally snaps and swears at the "waitress" in a little under thirteen minutes. The other "customers" win $100 for holding out past the fourteen minute deadline. If she is acting, then a very fine career as a movie star lies ahead of Ms. Germanotta if, or when, she wants to retire Gaga.

Left: Gaga pictured in October 2009 at the *Billboard* Women In Music event, New York.

"I want to be original more than anything. I don't really want to be like anyone. I want to be myself. I appreciate Madonna being provocative and not always about sex. It's not with me either."

ELECTRIC KISS

THE Conservatory at CAP21 is situated just above New York's Greenwich Village, in the heart of the Flatiron district. The faculty is six blocks south of the junction at 23rd Street where Broadway and Fifth Avenue cross, and where the famous Flatiron building sits. Ten blocks south is Washington Square, the setting for NYU buildings and the scene of one of the extraordinary spontaneous "happenings" that marked the Village folk movement, which spawned Bob Dylan and other folk heroes in the early 1960s. Every Sunday crowds of would-be folk singers gathered in the square to sing songs that they'd all know—or that they'd be willing to learn. Since that time the area has earned and kept a reputation for being the place for aspiring singer-songwriters and other artists in New York.

However, by the turn of the twenty-first century, the prices of apartments and condos in the Village had rocketed to such an extent that even long-established dives and rundown stores had been sold and developed, and subsequently transformed into multimillion dollar homes and upmarket stores, which were out of the reach of most of the people who lived there. This gentrification of the Village meant that the generally poorer artists and aspiring musicians were forced to move out of the area, and so they headed east—across the Bowery onto the Lower East side. A thriving community of clubs and bars soon grew up along Rivington, Delancey, and Grand, providing cheap beer, welcoming dark interiors, and small stages from which unknown bands and singers could reach out to a crowd who would usually number more friends than strangers.

It was among these cafes and clubs of the Lower East side that Stefani Germanotta

Name: Stefani Joanne Germanotta
Nickname: Stefi, The Germ
Usually seen: singing
Picture Her: without her midriff showing
Dream: headlining at Madison Square Garden
Reality: Cafe Casa
Male Equivalent: Boy George
Separated at Birth: Britney Spears
Prized Possession: her piano
Pet Peeve: "ordinary" people
Bet you didn't know: she was on *The Sopranos*
Didn't come to reunion: she had an audition

Opposite: Stef's entry in the Sacred Heart Yearbook in 2004.

developed a network of like-minded musicians and performers, many of whom became her friends. After her fame had begun to spread, footage of the eighteen-year-old Stef performing two songs at Ultraviolet Live, an annual talent show at NYU's Inter-Residential Hall Council in 2005, surfaced on YouTube.

The film shows the young Stef with long, very dark hair cascading over her shoulderless green top, worn with a silk, ankle-length white skirt and no shoes. She sings two self-written songs, entitled "Captivated" and "Electric Kiss" (which includes lines about changing the world with her lips). She is relaxed and is clearly enjoying

"I studied classical music, and I grew up hanging out in jazz clubs and being in jazz bands and choirs and rock and roll and stuff. So I was just surrounded by it growing up. I wasn't the girl that was hanging out with boys after school, you know? I was always doing something artistic."

her emotional performance. Given that the film shows Stefani with only the piano for accompaniment, it's quite hard to tell what the songs would sound like as performed by Lady Gaga, but Stefani Germanotta does a pretty good job with them. After she's finished, and earned rapturous applause, one of the contest judges, a woman named Bethane, praises Stef highly and announces that she's giving Stef's demo to "my publisher," before another judge proclaims, totally sincerely, "Norah Jones, look out!"

However, Stef only managed to come in third place in the talent show, behind second placed Funky Butter (a six-piece, 1970s'-style funk band with a female lead singer) and winners Tom Costello and Stephan Magloire—who promptly disappeared.

Ms. Germanotta's performance might not have been a winner that day, but it was enough to persuade Stef that her future might lie in being a pop performer rather than an actor in stage musicals.

Above: Luc Carl (right), Gaga's boyfriend from the Rivington Street days and manager of St. Jerome's bar, with Gaga collaborator DJ VH1, pictured here in 2007.

2

THE
GERM

During the summer of 2005, at the end of her first year at CAP21, Stefani was considering her next move. Performances she'd made as a solo singer-songwriter at concert halls and small venues had gone fairly well, but now there were three guys asking her to sing with their band. Living at home was proving to be a problem, because all her new friends lived down on the Lower East side and it wasn't hip to be from the Upper West side. Joe and Cynthia had been ecstatic when their eldest daughter had gained entry to the prestigious CAP21, and could see a career ahead of her as a stage actress and performer, possibly even a leading lady on Broadway. Yet, they'd also been appalled when Stef showed them her first tattoo, a small treble clef on her left hip, done when she was still seventeen. Cynthia cried then, so how would she react to the news that Stef was now building up to?

There was no way that Stef could continue to stay at the Pythian and live the life she was heading toward. She had her little sister to think about, too. Natali would be drawn into the world that Stef was now becoming immersed in, if they hung out together, and she was way too young for that. There was also Luc, the guy from the Lower East side who Stef loved, and wanted to be with.

With everything considered, Stef decided that it was time to drop out of college, move into a small apartment on Rivington Street and Suffolk—with Joe's support—and start a new life as a singer with a band. Those three guys liked her songs enough to name the act the SGBand. They had a small rehearsal place in a cellar under a grocery store close enough for Stef to wheel her Yamaha keyboard.

A new chapter in the eventful life of Stefani Germanotta, still known as "The Germ" to some of her old Sacred Heart crowd, was about to begin.

SOMETHING CRAZY

GUITARIST Calvin Pia and bassist Eli Silverman had been making music together with other friends for a couple of years and both were regularly gigging with different outfits—the most promising of which, Akudama, even set up its own MySpace site in June 2005—when they saw Stef perform. She'd seen them play and liked what she heard, which was a mixture of 1960s-style rock with country music-style harmonies, played with an indie rock sensibility. Pia and Silverman had a mutual friend named Alex Beckman who was a student at NYU and who played drums with a few different bands. He knew Stef from various events they'd both been in or performed at in her first year at CAP21.

In September 2005, with Stef having moved to and settled on Rivington Street, the four musicians—Pia, Silverman, Beckman, and Germanotta—began rehearsing. They played a mix of songs, some written by Stef and Calvin, along with classic rock numbers such as Led Zeppelin's "D'yer Mak'er" (a cod-reggae song from their *Houses of the Holy* album). Having decided to name themselves SGBand it was decided that all lead vocals would be handled by Stef. She began to favor a look recently made hip by the British singer Amy Winehouse. Piling her long black hair atop her head in as messy a bunch as possible, Stef would twine fake flowers into the strands which hung down almost to her waist. Unlike Winehouse though, who was still a relative unknown in America until her sophomore release *Back To Black* in 2006, Stef didn't go for revealing clothes on stage. SGBand were a "serious" indie band with alt-country roots that preferred to be included in such musical company as Wilco or REM. They were bands that had played their way to the top, touring and performing on the college circuits after breaking out of local college bars.

The SGBand soon began to pick up gigs in Lower East side bars such as The Bitter End and Mercury Lounge, where they developed a small but devoted fanbase. Among them was a music producer named Joe Vulpis, a commercial arranging graduate of Berklee College of Music '89, with a studio in New Jersey and music business contacts in L.A., Nashville, and New York. Stef persuaded the band to book some time in Vulpis's NJ studio in November 2005, and three months later they were selling the *Words* EP at gigs around New York. It's little more than a demo CD but shows Stef's obvious songwriting talent and distinct vocals. The five songs on the CD were "No Floods"—which she'd preformed live on NBC Channel 4 for the Columbus Day Parade in October 2005—"Something Crazy," which was also known as "When You're Not Around," "Red & Blue," "Wish You Were Here," and the title track.

And it was a recording at last.

Opposite (top): Gaga and Semi Precious Weapons' frontman Justin Tranter backstage at the Knitting Factory, New York, July 2007.

Opposite (bottom): The Bitter End club in Greenwich Village, New York.

> *"It never actually clicked for me in terms of art. I always knew I'd have a life in art. On my nineteenth birthday, I had gone to college for a year in musical theater. I think I was a little nervous about going out on my own after high school. It was like my family wouldn't let me take off. I was frowned upon in school to not go to college. Like I said, I was in theater training and I got a lot of 'You're too pop,' or 'You're too rock,' or 'You're too brunette.' 'You're a character, you're not an artist.' I'm a weird chick, you know?"*

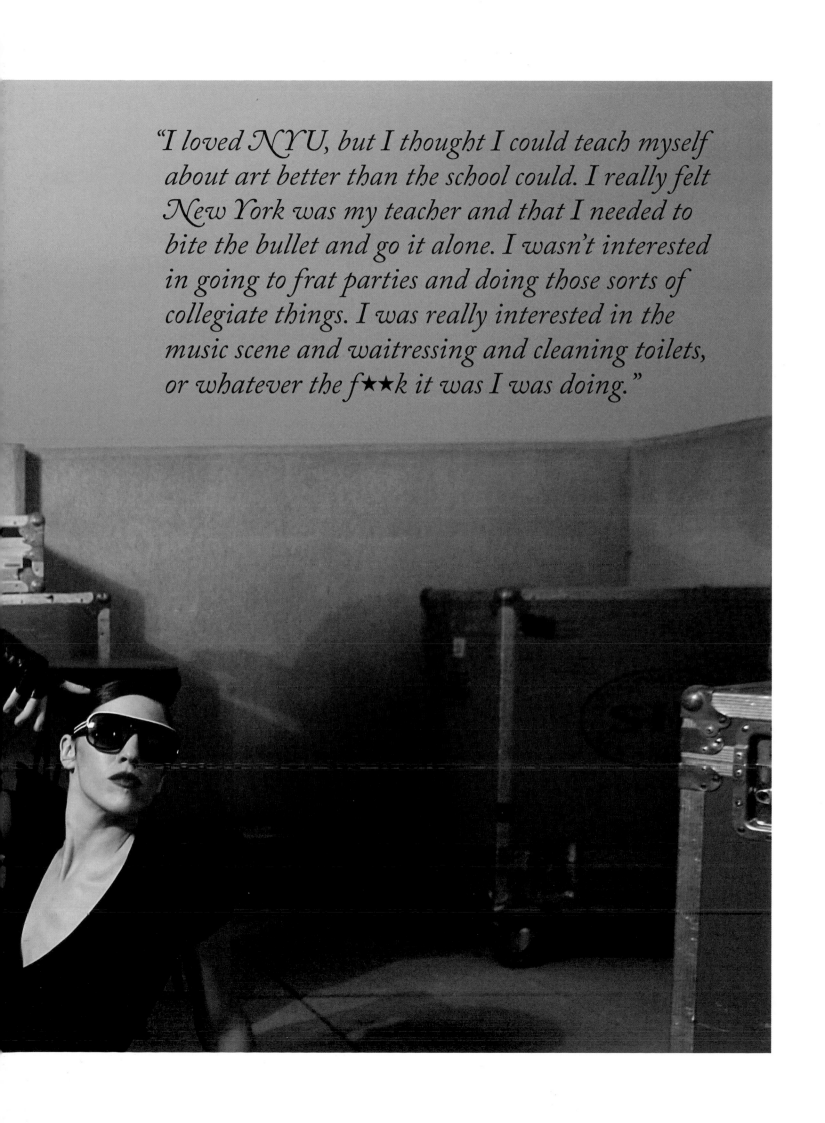

"I loved NYU, but I thought I could teach myself about art better than the school could. I really felt New York was my teacher and that I needed to bite the bullet and go it alone. I wasn't interested in going to frat parties and doing those sorts of collegiate things. I was really interested in the music scene and waitressing and cleaning toilets, or whatever the f★★k it was I was doing."

RED & BLUE

AFTER her first recording session, Stef knew that she had made the right decision in leaving home and college. She'd promised her parents that if she hadn't "made it" within a year she'd return to studying. The SGBand recorded a couple more songs, and impressed Joe Vulpis enough that he offered to release an EP for them in March 2006. The band had recorded two other songs along with the five for the demo—"Hollywood" and "Master Heartbreaker." They also had a few other numbers of their own that they'd perform, particularly "John's Song" and "Walk the Road."

The released EP would feature a re-recording and new arrangement of some of the songs from *Words*, though. "No Floods" was recorded with the whole band rather than just the piano and guitar version to be heard on *Words*. All of the songs—polished versions of those on *Words*—feature Stef's piano upfront in the mix and are mid-paced ballad-style rockers. There's not a hint of a dance beat anywhere on the recording, and it's only the voice that holds a clue as to the eventual emergence of Gaga from the performer at work on *Red and Blue*.

Having a CD for sale helped to get the SGBand more gigs, and they traveled as far afield as Pittsburgh, L.A., and Portland. It was while performing in New York though that Stef met someone who was about to change her life forever. A singing model named Wendy Starland who wrote songs and sang backing for a number of big stars was sent to watch the acts on the bill at the 2006 Songwriters Hall of Fame New Songwriters Showcase at The Cutting Room in June. She was there mainly because a New Jersey–based producer named Rob Fusari was looking for a female singer to front a new band that he was putting together and which would be kind of like The Strokes, only with a female singer (making them a new Blondie, in other words). Starland was there because Fusari couldn't be, but knew what he was looking for.

Stef appeared solo at the piano and performed her own song, "Hollywood." Starland was so blown away by the performance that when Stef left the stage she grabbed her and dragged her outside to call Fusari on a cell phone. He was asleep but woke swiftly when Starland shrieked that she'd found "the one" for him. Moving to his computer, Fusari called up Stef's webpage on PureVolume where he could hear some of her songs streamed. Despite being unimpressed by the songs, he could hear that she had "something" and so arranged for her to visit him at his studio in Parsippany, New Jersey, a few days later.

By this time it was clear that the SGBand were not going to get any bigger, and both Pia and Silverman were spending more time as part of Akudama anyway. Stef split the band and set herself ready to impress a big-name producer—Fusari had worked with Destiny's Child and Will Smith for *Wild Wild West*.

Since leaving the SGBand, Calvin Pia has remained a part of the indie alt-country act Akudama along with his brother Cayce on drums. Eli Silverman played bass for a short while, but they're now a trio led by Pia and Blake Charlton. Beckman went on to play drums with a trio named Brit and the Cavalry, fronted by another NYU Arts graduate named Brit Boras, the daughter of a classical cellist mother and jazz composer father.

Stefani Germanotta, meanwhile, was only weeks away from becoming a new person.

Previous page: Gaga takes New York, May 2008.

Opposite: Gaga asked photographer Angela Wieland to shoot some publicity images in July 2007. This image, along with those on pages 30 and 41, are from that session.

"On my nineteenth birthday, I just said, 'I'm going to get an apartment and a job.' My mother started crying. My father was like, 'If you don't make something happen within a year, you have to go back to school.' A year later, my production deal was signed, so I kept my word."

GAGA GODDESS
CYNDI LAUPER

SHE BOP

Rather than making comparisons between Gaga and Madonna, people would be better off and closer to the point in comparing Gaga to Cyndi Lauper—an arty New Yorker with a smart turn of phrase, outrageous dress sense, and uncompromising attitude to her music.

Cyndi Lauper was born in New York to an Italian-American mother and Swiss-German father in 1953. As a child she taught herself to play guitar and showed a wide artistic streak, which was fostered by her mother. After studying at a public school that specialized in arts and performance studies, at the age of seventeen Lauper left home in order to study art in Vermont. After college she returned to New York in order to sing in a rock and roll band. By the end of the 1970s—spent as a part of the New York arts scene that spawned punk and new wave—Lauper formed her own band named Blue Angel. In 1980 they released an album that failed to make any impact—and inevitably then split.

In 1981 Lauper was spotted singing solo in a small NY club by a music manager who signed her and got her a deal with a subsidiary of Epic Records (now Sony). With her original fashion sense, multi-colored hair, and incredible voice, Cyndi Lauper was always destined to become a star. That she did so as a fully fledged feminist was unique for the 1980s (and pretty unusual today). When songs were offered to her for inclusion on a debut record release, titled *She's So Unusual*, Lauper altered and rewrote the lyrics to fit her style. When she first read the words to what became "Girls Just Want to Have Fun" she thought they were sexist, so she changed them and created what became an international smash hit single in November 1983.

The follow-up release, "Time After Time," was also an international smash hit, and reached Number 1 in America on its release in June 1984. The third single from the album, titled "She Bop," made Number 3 in America in September the same year, despite implying onanistic practices. With her wild looks, hair, and makeup, her arty New York outlook and sense of fun, Lauper was irresistible to smart women (and men) who "got" that she wasn't at all trying to be like anyone else. She was a triumph of originality in a sea of impersonators trying to be the "new Madonna."

The makers of MAC makeup seem to have spotted the complimentary attitudes and mindset of Ms. Lauper and Lady Gaga. In February 2010 they launched a new anti-AIDS campaign for the MAC AIDS Fund, and a range of MAC lipsticks titled MAC VIVA GLAM, the profits from which go to the Fund.

Speaking at the launch of the lipsticks, Lauper said, "Lady Gaga and I are using our voices as a call to action for women all over the world. Each one of us needs to do our part to fight for women impacted by HIV and AIDS." For her part Gaga said, "Anything I can do to help raise money for HIV/AIDS awareness— that's what I'm here for, and I'm very honored to be a part of this."

Appearing onstage together in London with Sharon Osborne, the two stars looked as if they could be sisters. Both tottered on enormous spike heels, looking glam and gorgeous— Gaga in an enormous headpiece of bows with a mask over her eyes and lace bodysuit, Lauper in an exaggerated-shoulder-padded black jacket and her hair piled high and littered with jewels. They spoke intelligently and wittily about how women can reduce the threat of AIDS. At the U.S. launch Gaga performed for free, seated at a white piano, dressed in a white star-trooper outfit. The pair then appeared together on a string of TV talk shows to publicize the cause.

They looked a perfect couple and worked brilliantly together.

Opposite: Cyndi Lauper and Gaga at Salon Bordello, New York, November 2009.

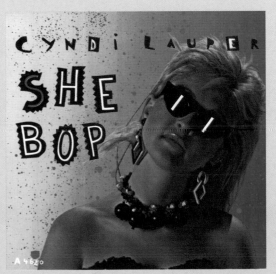

AGAIN AGAIN

FROM the moment Rob Fusari saw Stefani Germanotta he was . . . underwhelmed. She wasn't grungey enough for him, too clean-cut. But his friend Tom Kafafian persuaded Fusari to at least give her a chance since she'd traveled all the way from Manhattan. After a brief chat, during which Fusari heard nothing to make him change his mind, Stef sat at the piano and performed "Hollywood."

That changed Fusari's mind. She needed work, but he had time. It was soon clear that Stef was very happy to work with both Fusari and Kafafian, a songwriter, singer, and guitarist. Only Stef didn't have plenty of time. The deadline for the end of her make-or-break year was looming. She had only until college began again and if she wasn't making her way as a musician by then, Joe and Cynthia expected her to be back in classes when they began.

Stef traveled to New Jersey daily to work on songs she'd already written, and compose new ones. Her songs were too old fashioned for Fusari, although he thought she might be a rock performer, possibly in the Norah Jones mold. The problem was that nothing seemed to come out sounding special enough to do justice to either Stef or Fusari. So he encouraged her to be more dramatic. Stef was happy to oblige. Never more at home than when seated at a piano, she started goofing around with songs, singing falsetto in places, banging chords out with her fist in others. It all reminded Fusari of one of his favorite performers, Freddie Mercury, whose band Queen had released one of his favorite songs, "Radio Ga Ga." One day, while Stefani was messing about, Fusari told her she was "gaga" and from then on he'd sing snatches of "Radio Ga Ga" to her as they worked. One day he sent Stef a text that was meant to contain the title "Radio Gaga"

but for some reason—so the legend goes—the SMS was self-corrected to Lady Gaga. When she saw the name, Stef knew that it was perfect for her. She demanded from that day on that no one ever call her Stefani again; she was to be known only as Lady Gaga from then on.

By the end of the summer of 2006, though, neither Gaga nor Fusari were any closer to creating that something special they both knew they could. Then he had a radical idea. His greatest success had come via his work with dance and R&B artists (including Destiny's Child). There was no one out there making great pop dance music like Britney had once done, though. So, he asked Stef, what about if they drop the rock angle and make dance pop music instead?

It was a radical idea and one that needed a lunch at a Jersey branch of Chili's restaurant to persuade the former Stefani Germanotta to take up. Unconvinced about the change in musical direction Fusari was suggesting, she gave him the afternoon to persuade her that Lady Gaga could be a smash pop star instead of a rock one.

> "*Within 15 seconds, I'm like, 'This is it. My life is about to change.' While she's playing, I totally saw superstar potential. I just didn't know in what form or what genre it was going to be.*"

ROB FUSARI

TEAM LOVE CHILD

L ADY Gaga the newly minted pop artist and her producer Rob Fusari came up with a brand new song using a beatbox and synthesizer pretty quickly. It didn't sound like anything that SGBand would play, especially when Gaga performed it using her laptop to supply backing loops, while she played piano. Her new material sounded like nothing else that anyone on the club and bar circuit of the Lower East side was doing. Some of the early reactions from her indie friends were negatively critical. Naturally, it helped to persuade Gaga that she was on the right track with her new direction.

Setting up a company called Team Lovechild (the company with that name would eventually lead to a writ being served by Fusari on Gaga), Gaga and Fusari recorded and produced their new electro-beat pop tracks, and Fusari began playing them to music industry bosses. He was looking for a deal from both music publishers and record companies. Some people found the Gaga sound too unusual. Joshua Sarubin, the head of A&R at Island-Def Jam, thought it was interesting, though, and asked Gaga to come into his New York office and "audition" for him. He thought that her performance was unusual and provocative enough for the company to take a chance on her. When his boss Antonio "L.A." Reid agreed, they signed her on an artist development deal with the hope that they'd have an album ready for release within nine months. It was early September 2006 and Gaga had come in under the deadline for "making it." Or so she thought.

Late in September Gaga took the stage at The Cutting Room once more, dressed in a pink mini dress, knee-high white patent boots, and wearing her hair long, black, and straight. She performed "Wonderful" and "Fever" seated at the club's grand piano and earned loud applause for her performance. There was no beatbox or laptop, but she showed off a new tattoo on the inside of her left wrist; a Campaign for Nuclear Disarmament logo that had been adopted by the hippies as *the* symbol of peace at the end of the 1960s. Gaga had it inked in memory of John Lennon (who never actually used the symbol himself). She looked and sounded happy and relaxed on stage, telling everyone that she'd just signed a deal with Island-Def Jam.

But there followed three months of frustration. Despite Fusari introducing her to his managers at New Heights Entertainment, and their best efforts to progress the Def-Jam deal, Gaga couldn't get to talk to L.A. Reid about her music. She says she spent days sitting outside his office waiting to see him. Later she'd recall this period in her life as being a "dark" one, when she took drugs and came close to ruining her relationship with her parents.

As is often the case, though, out of adversity came triumph. When L.A. Reid decided that he'd made a mistake and dropped her, she found solace in her family. Just as Christmas 2006 was approaching Gaga was also dumped by the man who she thought was the love of her life. She was, she admitted, "pretty devastated", and moved back to the family home for the holidays. However, Gaga had recently made the acquaintance of someone new and inspiring. This new friend was to introduce Gaga to a whole other scene on the Lower East side and give her leads on a wholly different way of making and thinking about her music. She was also to become a performance partner to Gaga—and she too was a "Lady."

"I wanted to do something that was original and fresh. There's nothing more provocative than doing pop music in the underground, instead of doing underground music that would pass as pop. I'm talking about real pop music that would pass in the underground—the reverse. So I did that."

GAGA GOD
ANDY WARHOL

"It's all back to Warhol. I admire his ability to make commercial art that was taken seriously as fine art. That's my duty, I feel."

POPISM

In the mid-1960s one man did more than any other in establishing New York City as the epicenter of a vibrant, counter-culture art movement: Andy Warhol. A former advertising illustrator who became known for his blotted shoe drawings made in the late 1950s (he was born in 1928 in Pittsburgh), Warhol had also drawn LP record covers before his first one-man art show in 1962 made him an internationally renowned "fine" artist. Although his first show was in Los Angeles in July, his New York debut in November of the same year was more of a triumphant launch. On display were *Marilyn* (Monroe) *Diptychs*, *100 Soup Cans*, *Coke Bottles*, and *Dollar Bills*. These were not oil or watercolor representations of beautiful objects; the *Marilyn Diptych* was created from silk-screened publicity photographs. The soup cans were polymer paint reproductions of Campbell soup cans. Although ten years earlier British artists such as Eduardo Paolozzi and Richard Hamilton had used American magazine advertisements to create pop art collages, in America Andy Warhol was the vanguard of the "realist" school of pop art.

Warhol's use of everyday objects in his work, elevating the mundane to the level of high art, made it possible for anyone to be an "artist." Every aspect of life became a fit subject for Warhol's artistic interpretation. He made an eight-hour, black-and-white movie called *Empire* in which a static camera is trained on the Empire State Building, for instance, as well as a mere forty-five-minute movie called *Eat* in which a man eats a mushroom. Photographs of movie stars, pop stars, and gangsters taken from magazines were used as the basis for a series of screen-print works produced at Warhol's "Factory" by an army of Warhol helpers, hangers-on, and wannabes. It was all Art.

In 1963 Warhol opened his factory on East 47th Street and gathered around him an amazing array of cross-dressers, gay performance artists, musicians (he "managed" the band The Velvet Underground), actors, directors, poets, and socialites such as Edie Sedgwick whom Warhol claimed as his "muse." Fashion designer Halston also hung out at the Factory, which was often the scene of parties, impromptu performances, and exhibitions. Warhol named and created personas for many of his group, who became known as Warhol's Superstars. They adopted names that represented their aspirations to Hollywood-style fame such as Viva, Ultra-Violet, Candy Darling, and Baby Jane, and they dressed outrageously in multi-colored wigs, underwear as outerwear, couture dresses. They also sculpted outfits using everyday objects, and all wore high, high heels. Some of his superstars were transsexuals, most of his film stars were gay, all of them were artists.

In the 1970s Andy Warhol became a fixture at New York fashion shows and in the VIP rooms of the city's major discos such as Studio 54 and Palladium. He launched an expensive, large-format magazine titled *Interview*, which was all about celebrity culture (thirty years before the term existed). He mixed with emerging artists such as Basquiat and Herring, was never seen without someone rich, famous, and gorgeous—among them Elizabeth Taylor, Bianca Jagger, and Grace Jones—and never gave interviews to the press. He was always photographed wearing a platinum-blonde wig and dark glasses. He died in 1987 of heart failure following what was to be a routine gallbladder operation.

Warhol's influence and fame have grown every year since his death, to the point that everyone knows his name, if only because of his most famous quote, that "in the future everyone will be famous for fifteen minutes." Lady Gaga is clearly a big fan of the artist, filmmaker, fashion scion, photographer, and star-maker.

Opposite (top): Gaga with designers Richie Rich (left) and Traver Rains (right) at the launch of their Heatherette/MAC fashion collection, South Beach, Florida, March 2008.

Opposite (bottom): Andy Warhol with "Superstars" Ultra Violet (left) and Viva (right) in the late 1960s.

BEAUTIFUL DIRTY RICH

DURING the 1960s Andy Warhol and his Factory produced work that celebrated the underworld of New York. Drag queens, strippers, down and out poets, drug addicts, and porno stars became Warhol Superstars and established the NYC scene as the happening, cutting-edge, and seedy center of the art world. In some ways the idea of the Factory has never died in parts of New York. Artists and musicians have been attempting to recreate Warhol's scene in different parts of the city ever since Warhol passed away. By the time that Lady Gaga moved there, the Lower East side had become the latest area adopted by the artists and bohemians who lived their lives according to nonconformist rules.

As she watched some of the emerging cabaret-style burlesque acts who appeared at the bars and clubs she attended, Gaga figured that she should perhaps add an element of that to her show. In the wake of the disappointment of losing her record deal, Gaga began go-go dancing in bars owned by friends, usually dressed in little more than a glittering bikini. She started hanging out with a crowd of dancers, DJs, and performance artists who drew their inspiration from pop culture of the past. Besides the pre-WWII burlesque-influenced vaudevillean exotic dancers wearing their nipple tassels, stockings, and corsets, there were glammed up transsexuals dancing with beautiful performance artist-dancers. Lady Gaga got to know women and men who would only answer to their "stage names," which bore an uncanny resemblance to those adopted by Warhol's Superstars.

It felt to Gaga that she was becoming a part of a genuine scene, an underground movement that was fun, full of energy, ideas, and outrageous costumes. Her parents might not like it, but Gaga was having a ball. And it was about to become even more of a ball, one that glittered.

Opposite: Gaga performing at the "X your Ex" party, New York, Valentine's Day 2008.

Below: Gaga relaxing and watching a performance at St. Jerome's bar on the Lower East side, New York, June 2007.

"I was heavily immersed in that life, I was a scenester. I was partying in a particular lifestyle that everybody lived. It inspired me to try to understand what fame was really all about because we all felt so famous. None of us were. It was because of our love for our work, my love for the music, my love for the fashion, art, culture. Through that, you create an inner fame, and I duped a lot of people into thinking I was somebody that I wasn't. What I mean to say is I wasn't born into royalty, I had to earn it. I figured out a way to earn it."

3

ENTER
LADY

Mixing with the art crowd at NYU had taken Stefani further downtown and east than she'd been before. Now she was no longer answering to her given name, even to her parents. She was Gaga.

Opposite: Ladies Gaga and Starlight pose for a publicity shot, to be used on flyers for their upcoming performances together in 2007.

The clubs she used to play at age sixteen while her mom Cynthia acted as chaperone had grand pianos and roomy, clean stages. Now she was performing at clubs that were often little more than grimy cellars or bars with a cramped, slightly raised area for a stage and small house PA. This was a different New York nightlife to the one she'd first known. Some of the rich kids from uptown would slum it at places in the East Village on Avenues A and B at 7th and 8th Streets, but they didn't belong there.

Gaga was always different, though; the cross-dressers, drag queens, art students, and artists who traveled through tunnels and over bridges from Queens and Brooklyn for a truly special night out in the Lower East side felt like her kind of people. As with most things, she was absolutely right and meeting someone who was a soulmate, an innovator, mover, shaker, and trend-setting glam-girl DJ proved that. Her name was Lady Starlight and the first night that they met, Gaga put a ten dollar note into Starlight's bra, with her teeth.

Lady Starlight, a smart, Seventies-obsessed former art student, was at the forefront of the Lower East side performance art scene. A DJ, dancer, promoter and font of esoteric knowledge about the art scene which made New York great in the 1970s, Lady Starlight could—and would—teach lady Gaga a lot, not only about the kind of musical acts which Gaga hadn't heard her father play as she grew up, but also about the kind of cutting-edge, dramatic, brave entertainers and artists who inspired so many people into changing their lives. Just like Lady Gaga was changing hers.

GO GO AND THE STARLIGHT REVIEW

ɪɴ 2004 a female DJ approached the owner of a small bar in the East Village called Niagara at 112 Avenue A and asked for a chance to fill the downstairs tiki bar with various drag queens, exotic dancers, and wannabe glam stars. They said yes and gave the former SUNY student named Colleen, who had a huge love of English glam rock and street fashion, a Tuesday night slot. Black-and-white flyers bearing the words "Lady Starlight's English Disco" were duly distributed around the city.

The name was a nod to Rodney Biggenheimer's English Disco, which ran on Sunset Strip in L.A. from 1972 to '75; that had been the hippest place on the West coast at the time and only played glam rock—Bowie, Iggy Pop, New York Dolls, and T. Rex, many of whom would also perform gigs there when in L.A. Lady Starlight played the same vinyl records as Biggenheimer had. Among the crowd who flocked to her weekly Disco were similarly minded glam-lovers who wore vintage 1970s clothes and over-elaborate makeup, and who knew all the words to all the records that Lady Starlight played. The English Disco moved around—to Subtonic on Norfolk Street, for instance, and Niagara. After two years Starlight had gathered around her a gang of performers, dancers, and artists with similarly enigmatic "stage" names like Veronica

Vain and Anna Copacabana. They were very like Andy Warhol's Factory Superstars.

Later, Lady Starlight began spinning different kinds of beats at a different kind of club night. She was still into the glam scene, but she also loved the hard rock sound that underpinned much of the original glam records, and she gravitated toward hard rock music. Naturally, Starlight preferred English hard rock, and particularly that of Iron Maiden. Moving less than a dozen blocks south to Rivington Avenue, Lady Starlight got herself a gig as DJ for a metal-themed night, which she called Heavy Metal Soundhouse. Employing both Anna Copacabana and Veronica Vain as co-DJs, the three would also go-go dance in the dark, 1970s-styled bar, while tracks played loudly behind them.

It was here, in 2007, that she and Gaga met. As Lady Starlight describes the event, "When we met, she ran up to me and we instantly connected. Lady Gaga was in awe by what I was doing and asked me to be on stage with her. We then started blending ideas. At the time she was already working on her album and a lot of what's on *The Fame* were songs that we've performed. We worked on these acts for Lady Gaga and The Starlight Revue, which had Gaga rocking the keyboard and me on beats. We also did go-go

Below: Good times in boyfriend Luc's St. Jerome's bar, as Gaga shows her appreciation of Lady Starlight's go-go performance by stuffing a dollar bill into her brassiere with her teeth.

dancing and performances that featured disco balls and hairsprays being lit on fire."

Lady Gaga was soon going to the go-go dancing nights when Lady Starlight played records at St. Jerome's, Ming's (on Avenue B), and Coco66 in Brooklyn. Together they worked up a set featuring Gaga playing a synthesizer, which sequenced the backing tune to songs she and Rob Fusari were working on, while Lady Starlight spun vinyl records as backing beats. It didn't take long before the pair were

performing at places like The Bitter End, the Mercury Lounge, and the Knitting Factory on Leonard Street. These were hip, underground music joints and considered the starting place for future credible acts that would play art-punk, rock, and alternative sounds. Not many acts graduate from the Knitting Factory to become international pop stars. But then, Gaga wasn't taking inspiration from all the other indie bands playing the same venues. She was searching further back for her inspiration.

Above: Lady Starlight (sitting on the floor) and the English Disco set display their influences.

STARLIGHT REVIEW IN DAYLIGHT

I N the summer of 2007 Lady Gaga and Lady Starlight were booked to perform at an outdoor festival in Chicago called Lollapalooza. The festival had originally begun in 1991 as a vehicle for weirdo rockers Jane's Addiction, and what was to be a farewell tour with other weirdo buddies, among them self-piercing, tattooed circus freaks, thrash-metal bands, and fire eaters. It was to play at outdoor spaces, some of which had no seating or a proper stage.

By the time that Lady Gaga appeared sixteen years later on stage in a mirrored bikini top, short-shorts, and thigh-high boots alongside Lady Starlight in her DayGlo yellow bikini and Iron Maiden denim vest, the festival had become a "proper" event. It was now more of a family day out with kids accompanying Mom and Pop to the summer fun and frolics where they could browse the stalls selling official merchandise and cotton candy while bands played all day on stage. Lollapalooza had even appeared in an episode of *The Simpsons*.

The Lollapalooza festival offered wholesome music business-endorsed and supported entertainment, which is why Gaga earned her first police citation there, for public indecency. It was handed to her by a Chicago policeman before she got on stage. "There are children around here," he'd told her. Naturally, she was amazed.

"There's a huge festival with people doing drugs and he's busting me!"

Those people doing drugs were a minority of course, and blended with the crowd. Gaga stood out. For most of the crowd at the festival this was their first sight of the Lady in action, and it went down pretty well, even if she had "shocked" some of the crowd with her lack of clothing. There were doubtless hundreds if not thousands of people who went straight to her MySpace site on returning to their homes and

computers in order to hear what her recordings sounded like. She hadn't released any Lady Gaga music yet, but you could stream numbers via the MySpace site.

After the show, talking to a local reporter in her "daywear" of animal-print bikini, pink sequined belt, black spandex leggings, and black patent heels, she said, not for the last time, "I'm not really comfortable in a T-shirt and jeans." Drawing a comparison with an old David Bowie look, she continued to say that dressing down would be wrong, because "it would be like David Bowie doing Ziggy Stardust in a sweat suit—no one wants to see that."

While Lady Gaga and the Starlight Revue's show at Lollapalooza wasn't exactly Broadway theater, it was theatrical. A big mirrored disco ball was lowered into view as the Ladies performed, with each of them throwing Madonna-like "Vogue" poses as fake smoke drifted between them. Gaga danced around behind her synth and out front alone, posing, stretching, dancing, and prancing while Starlight spun two decks and posed away behind her. After coating their hair with aerosols they tried to set fire to a stream of spray—Lady Starlight got a rush of flames, but Gaga's didn't catch.

Gaga's performance must have seemed very theatrical among the otherwise straight guitar bands on the bill, which included Pearl Jam, Muse, and Iggy Pop. Intriguingly, the official Lollapalooza web site has no mention of Lady Gaga and the Starlight Revue as having appeared in 2007 (or any other year, either). It's as if the organizers want no connection with the biggest thing to happen in music in years. The experience can only have reinforced Gaga's conviction that playing pop music to supposedly underground, art, and alternative audiences was truly subversive.

Opposite: An incendiary set performed with Lady Starlight at Lollapalooza in Chicago, August 2007, saw Lady Gaga break out from the New York club scene.

"*Fashion and attitude and style, that's what we breathe for. It's a party. Everything my friends made fun of me for is what people want more of. More sequins, more spandex, yes please!*"

GAGA GOD
DAVID BOWIE

"I've always been into David Bowie. There's like an androgyny to my stage show. I'm super-feminine and sexy, but then again I sort of carry myself like a dude."

PRETTIEST STAR

In 1972 David Bowie took the music world by storm when he "became" Ziggy Stardust, an androgynous being from Mars with bright red hair, lots of makeup, and towering platform heels. After one hit single in 1969 ("Space Oddity") his career had stalled, despite having an album banned in both America and the UK because on the cover he appeared wearing a "dress." In fact it was an ornate, ankle-length coat designed by Mr. Fish, but because Bowie had shoulder-length blond hair at the time he looked, as he lay reclining on a sofa, like a woman (the album was called *The Man Who Sold the World*).

The album that launched Ziggy, titled *The Rise and Fall of Ziggy Stardust and the Spiders from Mars*, became a huge hit in England. The single taken from it, "Starman," made the Top Ten singles charts there, pushing the album to Number 5. Bowie toured America for the first time as Ziggy and began to make fans across the States late in 1972. A year later those fans bought his next album, the hugely influential *Aladdin Sane*. As the cover shows, it wasn't only the music which captured people's attention: the look was also significant.

When Lady Starlight began her English Disco at Niagara in 2004 she dressed as a perfect facsimile of David Bowie circa 1973/4, complete with bright red hair, eye patch, wide-lapeled blazer, platform shoes, and enormously flared trousers. That blue "lightning" streak Gaga wore on her cheek in 2008 as she promoted the single release of "Just Dance" is a reference to Bowie and a nod of thanks to Lady Starlight.

In 1972 Bowie also captured the attention of the world when he announced that he was openly bisexual. Posing with his wife Angie Bowie, who looked identical to David with her short blonde (soon to be dyed red) hair, high cheekbones, heels and similar clothes, the couple looked as if they'd landed from another planet. Statements of sexual deviancy were more shocking than unisex fashion back then. While there had certainly been many flamboyant performers, none had ever admitted their homosexuality for fear of being banned, castigated, and losing fans. Bowie helped to change all of that with his statement. Bowie broke so many rules and banished so many taboos that his influence stretched way beyond being just a rock star.

Throughout his career Bowie changed the way he looked and sounded almost with every new release. After *Aladdin Sane* and the follow-up album *Diamond Dogs* (1974), he did away with the brightly colored hair and makeup, swapping them for a 1930s-style strawberry blonde side bangs cut, baggy-fronted trousers, trilby hat, and sailor-striped T-shirt. He also swapped the sound of heavy guitars for funky ones on *Young Americans* (1975), a soul album (albeit one with a cover of the Beatles song "Across the Universe"), which includes the song "Fame," co-written with John Lennon and Puerto Rican guitarist Carlos Alomar.

It's easy to see—and hear—why Gaga so loves David Bowie.

"I was doing a lot of drugs when I wrote 'Dirty Rich' in about 2006, and it was about a few different things. First and foremost, whoever you are or where you live you can self-proclaim this inner fame based on your personal style, and your opinions about art and the world, despite being conscious of it. But it's also about how on the Lower East side, there were a lot of rich kids who did drugs and said that they were poor artists, so it's also a knock at that. 'Daddy I'm so sorry, I'm so, so sorry, yes, we just like to party.' I used to hear my friends on the phone with their parents, asking for money before they would go buy drugs."

STARSTRUCK AND STREAMLINED

WHILE Lady Gaga and Lady Starlight were wowing crowds with their alternative cabaret, producer Rob Fusari was busy working on the demos of songs that he had created with Gaga. Aware that another Jersey-based producer who he knew, named Vincent Herbert, was in the process of setting up his own record company, Fusari sent him a CD with some of the Team Lovechild tracks on it.

Herbert had enjoyed success with JoJo, whom he discovered and produced, and had worked as producer for Toni Braxton, Aaliyah, Whitney Houston, and—here's the Fusari connection—Destiny's Child.

Vince Herbert's company, which he'd named Streamline, had already signed the fourteen-year-old actor and singer Mishon, star of ABC's *Lincoln Heights*, for whom he'd produced and released via MySpace and YouTube their first song, "Excuse Me Mama." He was also looking at signing a Latin-Classical-R&B hybrid act called Madrigal, as well as an all-girl group to rival the Pussycat Dolls. As he saw it, Streamline was going to be all about "creativity without barriers." Which sounded just like something Gaga wanted, too.

Herbert liked the songs on the Fusari/Lady Gaga CD enough to attend a Gaga and Starlight Revue performance. As was their way the women performed wearing bikinis, dancing with glitterballs, and supported by back-up transvestite dancers.

Thankfully Herbert's reaction was somewhat more positive than that of Gaga's father Joe when he had previously caught a Starlight Revue. Where Joe had been shocked and rather embarrassed to see his daughter "cavorting" in an outfit which revealed possibly more than her underwear would, the unflappable record producer was more than impressed; he understood. Herbert told Gaga that he totally "got" her

and that he wanted to work with her. By the end of summer 2007 Lady Gaga had become a part of the Streamline roster. In early November 2007 Streamline announced a major development deal for the company with Interscope Records, the major rap label which had become a third of the Universal Music group (along with Geffen and A&M) in 1998. The official press release announcing the deal between the companies stated that Interscope would "provide promotion, marketing, and distribution for the multigenre label." That made Streamline a powerful player in the pop market.

As is usually the case when a record company signs an artist, the music publishing is the next deal to be made and so it was with Gaga, who signed directly with a major music business publisher, Sony/ATV. They, like Fusari and Herbert, felt that Gaga showed the potential to write great songs for other artists as well as for herself. It was their business to put songwriters together with recording artists and they set about placing Gaga's work for her. Interscope founder and boss of UMG, Jimmy Iovine, was also persuaded of Gaga's skills. Soon she was writing for a reformed New Kids on the Block and the Pussycat Dolls. Sony/ATV also asked if she'd be interested in writing for another superstar singer: Britney Spears. Of course she was.

As the year came to an end it seemed that things were, at last, happening for Gaga. With writing work for major artists on the horizon though, there was a chance that her own music performing career would suffer. She was meeting some of the music industry's most powerful people and impressing them, but not enough for there to be any firm immediate plans to make and release a Lady Gaga album. It was becoming clear to her that if she really wanted to be a part of the major music industry, then she'd have to leave her beloved New York and move as far west as possible.

Opposite: Lady Starlight and Lady Gaga backstage at the Rebel Club, New York, May 2007, at one of the first Lady Gaga/Lady Starlight Review performances.

"He (Joe) couldn't look at me for a few months. I was in a leather thong, so it was hard for him. He just didn't understand."

GAGA GOD
ELTON JOHN

DIRTY LITTLE GIRL

Just as Stefani Germanotta became Lady Gaga and conquered the world, forty years earlier Reg Dwight changed his name to Elton John and became a foot-stomping, piano-thumping, extravagantly attired, chart-topping pop star.

In the wake of David Bowie's success as Ziggy Stardust in 1972, and with the very pretty, glitter-dusted Marc Bolan having become the biggest star in the UK since the Beatles, pop stars had to dress in extravagant, colorful, and glittering outfits in order to succeed. In 1972 Elton had a world-wide hit single with "Rocket Man," a fairly slow ballad. However, it was swiftly followed by "Honky Cat," a much jumpier, funkier, and poppy hit single. While the album they came from (*Honky Château*) showed a slightly balding and bearded shot of Elton wearing dark glasses, the single sleeve for "Rocket Man" showed a very glam Elton in a white cowboy suit decorated with huge red roses (designed by extravagant Nashville-based designer Nudie) and an enormous cowboy hat similarly covered in roses. It was a hint of greater things to come. In February 1973 Elton scored his first American Number 1 single with "Crocodile Rock" and a year later he made Number 1 again with "Bennie and the Jets," taken from a double album titled *Goodbye Yellow Brick Road*, which also reached Number 1 in the *Billboard* album charts and includes the song "Dirty Little Girl" (it could almost have been written by Gaga!). The album cover shows an illustration of Elton in what were his trademark platform shoes shaped just like a grand piano—they look remarkably like a pair worn by Gaga at the 2010 Grammy Awards.

Elton's live shows in the early 1970s became over-the-top spectacles of explosions, flashing lights, and ever more extreme costumes. At different times he has appeared on stage wearing a diamante-encrusted baseball outfit; an all-in-one white catsuit—that is, shaped like a cat complete with whiskers and pointy ears; a Donald Duck suit from Disneyland; a Minnie Mouse costume; in a pink suit with a replica of the Eiffel Tower as a hat; in an all-feathered, winged suit and hat; and in a golden Space-age, ornately carved cat suit topped by extravagant spectacles, which spell the word "zoom." He has also been photographed wearing an elaborate French Revolution-era

silver wig, frock coat, and bejeweled cane, a Russian General's outfit with glittering medals and, of course, lots and lots of designer suits. He was friends with Gianni Versace, Princess Diana, and is now a "Sir," having been knighted by the Queen of England.

Nobody should have been surprised when Lady Gaga and Sir Elton performed a duet together at the Grammy Awards ceremony of 2010. They sat at pianos opposite each other, both wearing sparkling glasses with make-up smeared faces. Elton wore a large dangling Gaga-like earring while her shoulder pads looked as if they'd been torn from a quarterback and sprayed with glitter. They performed a mashup of her "Speechless" and his "Your Song," singing at each other among a forest of mannequin arms stuck on top of the pianos. In an interview after the show, Sir Elton said of his co-star, "She's the only exciting thing out there in music at the moment. She's so organized and has her own vision, I'm so impressed with her."

Above: Elton in iconic form, 1974.

Opposite: Gaga and Elton get dirty at the Grammy Awards, January, 2010.

BYE
BYE
BABY

As the year 2007 came to a close, Lady Gaga began to make plans to visit—indefinitely—Los Angeles, California. Vincent Herbert was living out there and had an office near to Interscope headquarters in Santa Monica. There were plans for Gaga to meet with and hopefully work for ace R&B singer/rapper Akon, whose own label, Konvict, was hoping to break some new artists. He'd been introduced to Gaga's music by another producer under the same management as Gaga (New Heights), who in turn was waiting to work with her. His name was RedOne, and he'd be in a studio in L.A. waiting for the Lady on her arrival early in the New Year. Plus, the already established artists who Gaga was to write songs for were mostly based in L.A.

So, with some regrets Gaga set about organizing her new life in California. In some ways it would do her good to get away from New York for a while. Over the previous six months her hectic schedule of writing, performing, dancing, and living down on the Lower East side had been almost too much fun—Gaga had picked up some bad habits. Thankfully she wasn't too badly into anything addictive. As her career looked like taking off she knew that she had to do something about it, though. As at many crucial points in her life, Gaga's mind was finally made up about cleaning up when she realized that her father knew she was high. As she later told an interviewer, "My father—I never told him what I was doing and he knew. He looked at me and just said, 'You're f★★king up, kid.' I was so mortified that my father would see that weakness in me. As an artist, I'm fascinated with the nostalgia and what it meant in the '70s and how artists went on creative journeys using narcotics. That's why I did it. I didn't do it because I wanted to get high. I did it because I wanted to find my creativity. It wasn't until I discovered it was a weakness . . . I just said, 'The hell with it.'"

With the emotional support of her Lower East side friends and her family, Gaga stopped with the drugs and concentrated on working out new looks to go with her new music. The scene had been so vibrant and stimulating that Gaga had to find a way of taking some of it with her. Always eager to give credit where it was due there was no way that Lady Gaga would forget about Lady Starlight, Ana Copacabana, Veronica Vain, Breedlove, or Matty Dada.

Opposite: Gaga as we know her emerged at the Slipper Room, New York, October 4, 2007. This was her first performance as a blond; the show was one of her last in New York before she moved to Los Angeles.

Below: Friends Gaga and Starlight together again, here at the party after the MTV Video Music Awards, New York, September 2009.

JUST DANCE

THE day that her plane touched down at LAX, Lady Gaga was carrying a hang-over from her farewell party of the pre-vious night. Yet she couldn't wait to get to work with RedOne and so went straight to the studio to meet him. Although born and raised in Morocco, RedOne (real name Nadir Khayat, see page 78) had grown up obsessed with Western pop music and had created for himself a signature Eurobeat sound. It was a step further into pop music than Rob Fusari had gone, and it was to prove to be a very big one for Gaga.

According to Gaga and RedOne it took no longer than the day to write and record the basic track for "Just Dance." Later Vince Herbert would claim that Gaga wrote the whole of her debut album *Fame* in ten days. It wasn't true—some of the songs on it had been written with Rob Fusari in 2007—but it seemed as if she worked fast because she had done so much work in the build-up to making the album. Some songs were already partly formed when she started work on them with RedOne.

"Just Dance" is as catchy as can be and includes a middle-section rap by one of Akon's protégés, Colby O'Donis (plus vocals from Akon who also gets a writing credit). It was a natural choice as her first single, but it wasn't an instant hit.

Released in April 2008, "Just Dance" was promoted as a dance track in clubs and had no less than twelve remixes released on different CDs and as separate downloads. The video that accompanied the release featured Gaga at a party dressed in hot pants with a Bowie-like blue flash on her cheek, her hair a platinum blonde, her bikini-style top made of reflec-tive mirrors. In another nod to her NY friends

Gaga dances with the mirrored disco ball that she and Lady Starlight used on stage, while the party DJ spins 1970s-era vinyl (including Blondie's *Greatest Hits*). Gaga changes her out-fits throughout the video, of course, and at one point is seated astride an inflatable whale in a child's paddling pool.

The video was great fun to make, she later recalled: "It was like being on a Martin Scorsese set. I've been so low budget for so long, and to have this incredibly amazing video was really very humbling. It was really fun. That video was a vision of mine. It was Melina [Matsoukas] the director who wanted to do something, to have a performance art aspect that was so pop but it was still commercial, but that felt like lifestyle. It was all those things, I love it."

Despite being so unusual and attention-grabbing though, while "Just Dance" would eventually make the Number 1 spot in countries around the world, it would take a lot of hard physical work by Lady Gaga to get it there. But she was never afraid of hard work.

"It took me eight years of pining and pining and sweating and believing and scraping at the marrow in my bones for the right sound until I finally found it. I wrote "Just Dance,' and it finally happened. It's like giving birth. It's immaculate conception. It saved my life."

4

GO
GAGA

Once settled in Los Angeles, Lady Gaga found herself working nearly all of the time in studios with different singers (Akon, Colby O'Donis, Nicole Scherzinger), producers (RedOne, Vincent Herbert, Darkchild), and writers (Martin Kierszenbaum). She had a handful of songs that she and producer RedOne were working up and complimenting with new numbers, which they had great fun putting together. Her publishing company were pushing her talents as a writer for other people, pretty much all of who were big stars. Meanwhile Akon was working with her on songs for artists signed to his own label.

Those early months out west were all about getting the Gaga name known on the L.A. music scene. Friends helped a lot, and some of her buddies from back east—particularly Matty Williams—traveled out to see her, then stayed and became a part of project Gaga. Matty moved in with her and soon the Gaga residence became known among friends as the "house of Gaga." Inspired by her art and fashion background, Gaga adopted the German spelling of Haus and created a whole new company, which employed Matty—now known as "Dada"—and choreographer Laurie-Ann Gibson (L.A.G.) to help create the essential Gaga look and steer its artistic direction. Haus of Gaga would from now on be credited on everything that the Lady did, and employees of the Haus would always be by her side to help, advise, and direct everything, from photo shoots and video filming to choosing what items would make great props and parts of a costume design.

It wasn't exactly the Lower East side, but the Gaga posse brought a little bit of New York sassiness, attitude, and invention to sunny Los Angeles. She wasn't a star yet, but that didn't mean that she had to act as if she weren't famous. Gaga's notion of fame had little to do with who knew about her, after all.

Previous page: Gaga onstage during the MTV Video Music Awards, New York, September 2009.

Opposite: Gaga performs at the party to launch issue 61 of V magazine, which featured her on the cover (see page 87).

I
GET
AROUND

SOON after Akon had hired Gaga to work with him on creating songs for one of his own fledgling acts, a Jamaican former backing singer to Shaggy named Tami Chynn, he realized that Gaga could be as big if not bigger than Tami. In return for helping Gaga with her career, Akon formed a distribution contract for her through Interscope (Streamline remained part of the deal) and then pushed her talents as a performer to Jimmy Iovine and Interscope in general.

Gaga was hired by Iovine to write songs for the long-delayed solo album by Pussycat Dolls lead singer Nicole Scherzinger (unreleased at time of writing). They put Nicole together with RedOne who of course knew how best Gaga worked, and together they set to creating songs for the Doll. However, after two years of trying, Interscope had still not managed to create an album of songs for Nicole that were as strong as those that had made the Pussycat Dolls such big stars. Or perhaps the Dolls took precedence because they were so big—and were totally and completely "owned" by Interscope: the Dolls were employees of the record label who paid them a wage and ensured that they were each, except Nicole, replaceable.

With a second Dolls album slated for release in September 2008, Gaga was asked to write for them, too. Although in the end they didn't record any of her songs, she impressed them and Iovine enough that they would all work together again in the future. Meanwhile, Iovine had signed the recently re-formed boy band New Kids on the Block and had them working with RedOne, among other producers. Gaga was asked if she'd want to work with the Kids and she couldn't say "no" to that. With RedOne behind the desk she recorded a guest vocal on a track titled "Big Girl Now" and had one of her songs, co-written with

RedOne and Donnie Wahlberg and titled "Full Service," included on the album, too.

All the time spent in the studio working with other artists, especially ones with vast experience like NKOTB, can't have helped but rub off on Gaga. Smart enough to learn from her experiences and quick enough to adapt her own working practices, Gaga's writing went from strength to strength. While she was working with RedOne, Akon, New Kids, and Nicole, Sony/ATV called to let her know that a couple of her songs had been chosen by Britney Spears. She chose to record just one song, "Quicksand," and it only appeared as an iTunes bonus track in the European market, but still; it was Britney, one of Gaga's early musical heroes.

By April 2008 Gaga was becoming very well known in pop circles as a good songwriter. Her next move was to become better known as a great pop music performer and a recording artist. The release of "Just Dance" would begin that process. Or so she hoped.

Above (L-R): Akon, Doug Morris (CEO of Universal Music), Gaga, and Jimmy Iovine (Chairman of Interscope, Geffen, and A&M Records) at a launch party December 2009, New York.

Opposite: Akon, Gaga, and her father, Joe, attend the Grammy Awards, January 2010, Los Angeles.

"There's something very humbling about writing for a powerhouse group like Pussycat Dolls. Every time that you work with somebody that's better than you are, you become greater."

GAGA GOD
FREDDIE MERCURY

"Equating oneself with royalty is such a female thing to do. We dress up as princesses and queens and we wear crowns, but Freddie created this image of himself as rock royalty. That performance screams, 'Watch me! I'm a legend!'"

KILLER QUEEN

Like many of Gaga's fave musical inspirations from pop's glittering past, Freddie Mercury of Queen changed his name in order to succeed. He was born in Tanzania to Indian parents and named Farrokh Bulsara. He was sent to a private boarding school in Mumbai at age eight, and his family moved to England when Farrokh—who was already calling himself Freddie—was seventeen. After attending art school he joined a few bands and sold second-hand clothes in a hip West London market. When he was twenty-four he met guitarist Brian May and drummer Roger Taylor, and together with bassist John Deacon they formed Queen in 1970. Apparently, Freddie did know that the name had gay connotations.

From the beginning of his career Freddie Mercury was theatrical and colorful onstage and off. He mixed as many musical genres and looks into Queen as he could. "I hate doing the same thing again and again," he told one interviewer, adding that he liked to take influences from "music, film, and theater."

While she took her name from the song "Radio Gaga," it's not the obvious Queen number that one would associate with Lady Gaga. The six-minute mini opera that is "Bohemian Rhapsody," with its pitch and time changes, theatrical pomp, and ground-breaking video, could be a great Gaga cover song. As could "Killer Queen," perhaps, or even "Fat Bottomed Girls." But it's not the music Gaga loves so much as Freddie himself and particularly his image; as she explains, "When he's in the king's outfit, with the scepter."

The self-confidence and determination that Freddie exhibited in rising to the top of the

music business when he did offers much to be admired. It wasn't until long after he had been famous as Freddie Mercury that anyone realized either that he was Indian or that he was gay . . . even when he appeared wearing a tight white vest and "clone" moustache. That is partly because Freddie considered it nobody's business but his own, and partly because his band was creating heavy rock guitar albums and anthemic songs such as "We Are the Champions." He must have loved to hear crowds of macho, homophobic soccer thugs singing his song at matches; they were not being ironic when they sang it, either.

Freddie's attitude of showmanship, defiance, and professionalism appeals to Lady Gaga. And after all, she's almost royalty herself.

Above: Gaga bows to Queen Elizabeth II following the Royal Variety Performance, December 2009, Blackpool, England.

Opposite: The King of Queen in 1985.

CHERRY CHERRY BOOM BOOM

By the time that "Just Dance" was ready for release in April 2008, Lady Gaga was situated firmly within a family of people who would help her to become an international star. New members of this "family" were Interscope A&R chief Martin Kierszenbaum who was to help Gaga write new songs, and English DJ Space Cowboy who would become an important part of the Haus and Gaga's performance when on tour.

Kierszenbaum (whose nickname is Cherry Cherry Boom Boom) was not only a co-head of A&R (with Iovine) but also had his own label, Cherrytree Records, which was a part of Interscope. Adding to the already convoluted Gaga label situation, Kierszenbaum had to have his label logo attached to any material he wrote, produced, or promoted, and so Gaga was now "signed" to Streamline, Konvict, and Cherrytree all at the same time, with parent company Interscope overseeing everything. At least she was working personally with the bosses of each company, and so was assured of first-class treatment by the label.

Kierszenbaum had risen to prominence at Interscope as a kind of international A&R scout. He had discovered and broken the Russian "lesbian" act t.A.T.u. in 2002 when he co-wrote their international hit "All the Things She Said." By recording them singing in English and managing their public appearances (they publicly kissed one another whenever a camera was pointed at them), Kierszenbaum gave t.A.T.u a Top 20 American hit and put them into the Top 10 around the world with the single and the follow-up album *200k/h in the Wrong Lane*. Kierszenbaum also signed the Canadian artist Feist, and she subsequently increased her fanbase around the world with the album *The Reminder* (2007), as have many other acts who worked with Kierszenbaum, including Swedish pop star Robyn. Like RedOne, Kierszenbaum knew what was happening in the charts in Europe as well as America, and he knew that any act had to be a hit around the world if they wanted to be truly successful. Which is why the songs he wrote with Gaga—"Eh Eh (Nothing Else I Can Say)," "The Fame," "I Like It Rough," "Starstruck," and "Christmas Tree"—are driven by a Eurodisco beat.

Set on global dominance, Lady Gaga was happy to undertake a trip around the world, beginning in May 2008, to promote the release of "Just Dance." For the first two months she appeared with NY buddy DJ VH1 and two backing dancers, making personal appearances at clubs, bars, and conference events across America. In July she flew to Berlin for a fashion event, then to Canada, and had another sweep across America throughout August. At the end of August and all through September Gaga got to visit Europe and Australia.

Some of the shows Gaga appeared on were broadcast over the radio, and some were televised. All were important in getting people to see Lady Gaga in action. Usually she would sing four songs, mostly "Beautiful, Dirty, Rich," "Paparazzi," "LoveGame," and "Just Dance," but she sometimes performed "Lovestruck," "Poker Face," and "Eh Eh," too. She would always get to sing "Just Dance," and show off her amazing outfits and attitude. DJs, promoters, and club goers from Hollywood to New York via Vegas, Texas, Chicago, and Florida were among the first people outside of the Lower East side to get a good look at a rapidly evolving superstar.

Opposite: Gaga with Space Cowboy and dancers at the Open A.I.R. Summer Concert, New York, May 2008.

"I hate the feeling when I'm at a nightclub and an artist is performing to a track with a mic in their hand, and a bored look on their face. I'm not interested in 'auditioning' for the world. I'm not wasting time."

REDONE

ʙᴏʀɴ Nadir Khayat in Morocco in 1974, the youngest of a large family, the man who became RedOne grew up surrounded by American and Western rock music. He had the record collections of his older siblings to listen to, which included Springsteen, Led Zeppelin, David Bowie, and the big names of the 1970s. As a teenager he became a fan of the Swedish rock bands Europe and Roxette, and played rock guitar in local bands. In the mid-1990s he got the chance to move to Sweden and, after a year or so playing guitar, began jobbing in studios in Stockholm. So began the fourteen years in which he worked hard and learned how to add the by-then well-established Eurobeat backing to pop songs by a range of bands. In 2001 he worked as producer for A-Teens (a former ABBA teen tribute act) with some local success. RedOne really broke big in Sweden with Darin, the runner-up of Sweden's *Pop Idol* in 2004, and continued to work with him even after moving to America.

RedOne moved to America in order to work with R&B acts after composing and creating the theme song for the 2006 FIFA World Cup tournament, titled "Bamboo." However, at first work was scarce, and he found himself and his wife planning a return to Sweden unless something came along in the first three months of 2007. Luckily he was offered the chance to produce Kat DeLuna and after "Whine Up" and *9 Lives* were a hit, RedOne became a known producer in the States and received offers of work

from a wide range of labels. After scoring a hit with Kat DeLuna, RedOne told his manager that he only wanted to work with signed artists from now on—but was then introduced to Gaga just after she'd been dropped by Def Jam, and before she'd signed with Streamline. However, as he tells the story, they got talking about music and he said, "Let's go to the studio and try some things out." They did and almost instantly came up with the song "Boys Boys Boys."

Working with Akon and on the New Kids on the Block comeback album meant that RedOne had the opportunity to involve Gaga with both artists, to the delight of all involved. Had Michael Jackson lived, then there is every chance that Gaga could have made a guest appearance on the album he was making, with RedOne producing, at the time of his death.

Gaga and RedOne clearly have a sympathetic approach to making music. As RedOne told one interviewer, "Gaga writes and I produce and write so we don't need anyone else, honestly. Me and her, we're just magic. It just flows." Their mutual love for metal and rock sounds has produced a body of songs that can sound—indeed have sounded—just as good when played by a classic guitar-bass-drums band. Within weeks of "Just Dance" becoming a hit, YouTube hosted cover versions of the song played by a variety of indie bands. New cover versions of that and other Gaga/RedOne numbers are regularly added to the site. Proof that great songs work in any musical style.

"RedOne is like the heart and soul of my universe. I met him and he completely, one hundred and fifty thousand percent, wrapped his arms around my talent, and it was like we needed to work together. He has been a pioneer for the Haus of Gaga and his influence on me has been tremendous. I really couldn't have done it without him. He taught me in his own way—even though he's not a writer, he's a producer—he taught me how to be a better writer, because I started to think about melodies in a different way."

"It's not a persona, it's me in all my origami glory. That's sort of the whole idea. I'm a performance artist. I've been doing performance art in New York since I was 19 years old. I make the fashion, I write all the music, all the visuals that you see in the show, I designed. I dress like this all the time. It's not a look. I live and breathe it, and if they took my origami away, I would be kicking and screaming to my coffin."

GAGA GOD LEIGH BOWERY

LIVING ART

When Lady Gaga says she loved Boy George, she is paying tribute—perhaps unknowingly—to an Australian performance-artist-designer-pop star of the 1980s and '90s called Leigh Bowery. As founder and master of the hippest underground club in 1980s' London (Taboo), Bowery created the kind of fashion as living art statement that first Boy George and now Gaga have taken to wider audiences.

Originally from the improbably named Sunshine, Australia, Bowery traveled to London as an ex-art student in 1980. There, separately from the emerging New Romantic scene of the time, Bowery began to appear in public wearing amazing one-off creations that would often involve cross-dressing elements, full-body bright coloring, exaggerated lipstick, and head-wear made from odd items—saucepans, telephones, fish, eggs, seaweed.

Leigh Bowery was a big man who grew even bigger—he was able to wear bras without needing to pad them—and exaggerated his size by wearing enormous platform shoes and padding his clothes (one outfit had shoulder pads that rose to the top of his bald head). Most of Bowery's fashion creations involved covering his face, often with paint, and wearing oversized eyelashes, polka-dots or mirrored-helmets. He wore all-in-one body suits made from sofa fabric. One made him look like a comic-book ghost with no face, another had fixed flared legs that covered his platform shoes as well as every inch of his body.

As well as running Taboo—where there were no rules—Bowery also sat for renowned artist Lucien Freud and is the subject of several well-known and expensive Freud works. Bowery also collaborated with British ballet dancer and choreographer Michael Clark to create costumes—usually based on those he'd wear at clubs—and "dancing" in works staged at theaters and art centers across Europe.

Leigh Bowery was a huge inspiration to others. Designer Rifat Ozbek not only knew him, but worked with him, taking some of Bowery's design elements into his own work. Similarly, corsetiere Mr. Pearl and milliner Philip Treacy created items of which Bowery would approve. As befits an individualist like Bowery, all of his creations were one-offs, and he didn't want to create fashions for other people.

Bowery formed two bands, neither of which were ever successful. The first, Raw Sewage, was made up of Bowery and two drag artists who wore typically bizarre Bowery creations, which they'd take off during live performances, so ending with all three naked, except for face masks. Bowery insisted that the trio sing live and didn't lip synch while they covered Run DMC's "Walk This Way." His second "band" was called Minty and they did manage to score a club hit in Holland, with a song titled "Useless Man."

One of his collaborators described Bowery as being a "beautified monster," and that monster aspect is carried through to Gaga's extraordinary fashion statements, all of which are one-offs, created for a performance by her and the Haus. The link between Bowery and Gaga was Alexander McQueen, who as a young fashion student in London in the early 1990s attended as many of Bowery's fashion shows, art performances, and gigs as he could.

Sadly Leigh Bowery died, of AIDS-related illness, in 1994.

Opposite: Gaga at a New York Fashion Week event, February 2010.

Below: Leigh Bowery in 1985.

GAY GAGA

Sprinkled liberally among the club dates that Lady Gaga undertook to promote "Just Dance" in the summer of 2008 were numerous gay clubs and gay-night events at other clubs. With her roots in the cross-dressing gay revue bars of the Lower East side, Gaga had developed a strong and sympathetic gay following from the moment she began go-go dancing with Lady Starlight. Her cutting-edge fashion sense and love of over-the-top outfits added to her appeal among the sartorially extravagant club-goers who, since the 1980s, have found a vibrant and tolerant audience at gay clubs.

It has been a music business working practice for some years to "break" dance and pop acts by booking them into PAs at gay clubs across the country. Special mixes of singles are released to gay clubs only, with the kind of heavy bpm (beats per minute) that Gaga and RedOne naturally include in their work, in order to spread the word on new acts. With her intriguing look and dance music, Gaga was always going to be a hit with some clubbers, particularly those who appreciate sassiness and effort put into a look.

Gaga looked forward to performing in gay clubs because, as she explained in a Q&A interview with *Rolling Stone* magazine, when she was

Below: A Gaga charity concert for people living with HIV, Tokyo, April 2010.

Left: Gaga addresses
thousands of activists
gathered on Capitol Hill
to demand equal rights
during the Equality
March in Washington,
DC, October 2009.

starting out, "I was in New York, partying a lot at gay clubs and dive bars. I was out five nights a week [and] fell in love with the Cure, the Pet Shop Boys, the Scissor Sisters. I got really fascinated with eighties club culture." That eighties club culture was all the rage in gay clubs, and has helped some stars of the previous era resurrect dormant careers—among them another Gaga goddess, Grace Jones (see page 91).

Coming from New York meant that Gaga was possibly unaware of the possibility that aspects of liberal society could still cause uproar in more conservative parts of America. "I had a few gay piano teachers," she recalled later in an interview with a gay publication, adding that "I was in acting class and ballet from a very young age, and I remember being around a lot of gay boys in dance class. I feel intrinsically inclined toward a more gay lifestyle."

So it was natural that Gaga should appear at various Gay Pride events that summer, including the big San Francisco Pride Party for Everyone on June 28. Not that she was eager to be seen to exploit either her gay fans nor her own involvement in the gay scene in New York.

Despite the fact that "Boys Boys Boys" was one of the first songs ready for release, she didn't want it released simply because it could be turned into a camp gay anthem. Not because, as she explained, that she didn't want to have a gay anthem hit, since she'd be very happy if all of her songs were. Rather it was too obvious a move to release it first. In an interview about the matter Gaga was typically contentious, stating, "The real motivation is to turn the world gay."

More than a year after appearing at the SF Pride Party, Gaga would sing a slightly altered version of John Lennon's "Imagine" at the Human Rights Campaign National Dinner, in order to help publicize Gay Rights. She even dressed down in order to get her very serious message across.

Amid all the PR hype that Gaga was generating in order to sell her music, she maintained her focus and demonstrated what was most important to her. It wasn't just about selling her music, although with her debut album released in August 2008, *Fame* would become the new Gaga mantra; Gaga wanted to do good work in charitable areas, too.

"When I started in the mainstream it was the gays that lifted me up, I committed myself to them and they committed themselves to me, and because of the gay community I'm where I am today."

TURN
TO
THE
LEFT

FROM the moment that Elvis Presley made his groundbreaking appearance on the *Ed Sullivan Show* in 1955, rock 'n' roll and fashion have been constant and ever-evolving companions. A great look has been as important as a great song for many pop stars—and for some artists the look has been more lasting than their music—for the past six decades. Once in every generation of performers comes an entertainer who stretches, challenges, and ultimately changes the way in which the music is presented. After Elvis, the Beatles made sure that any boy with a design on hip girls grew a moptop. David Bowie not

only inspired a generation of men to dye and spike their hair, but also to change their clothes from flares and T-shirts to suits with shoulder pads (and he had a huge hit with a song titled "Fashion," too).

As rock and pop music expanded and grew, so too did the appearance and the cut of musicians' clothes. Many artists with great individual looks have been cited by Gaga as inspirations. The designers behind their looks have also been namechecked by the Lady. Among the fashion designers that she loves the most are Gaultier, Versace, Dior, Muegler, Westwood, and McQueen.

Gaga as fashion leader and model. Opposite, below, and top left following page: Gaga worked with photographer Mario Testino for the cover and interior of the fall 2009 issue of V magazine.

Following pages, bottom left: U.S. *Elle* magazine, January 2010; top and bottom right: Italian *Max* magazine, December 2009.

"*The fashion, the technology, and just being innovative with what people are hearing and seeing are a big aspect of my music. I want people to go to my show going 'What the f★★k was that!?' In other words it's like a pop show fit for a museum.*"

MAGAZINE

FALL FASHION WITH LINDA KATE AMBER AND NAOMI!

PLUS: SWEDISH ROCK NEW YORK LEGENDS ART IN VENICE

IT'S LADY GAGA'S WORLD

...WE'RE JUST LIVING IN IT!

LADY GAGA IN MARC JACOBS COAT AND GLASSES PHOTOGRAPHED BY MARIO TESTINO

61

FALL 2009

US $6.50 CAN $7.50 DISPLAY UNTIL NOVEMBER 1, 2009

It is the year's most inescapable song. From the "Mum mum mum mah" robo-Gregorian chant of the opening to the slinky verse to the singsong hook—it's 2009's "I Kissed a Girl," "Since You've Been Gone," and "Womanizer" rolled into one, at once slinkier and smarter than all three. It's one of those tunes against which resistance is futile. Even rockers like the Arctic Monkeys, Weezer, and Faith No More have busted out their own versions this year, much to Gaga's delight.

"I looove Faith No More! Their song 'Epic' was my burlesque number at the bar I used to work at! I used to fog myself and dance to it. When I found out they did 'Poker Face,' I was like, Shit!" Of course, it's not Faith No More, nor influences David Bowie, Queen, or the Cure to whom Gaga is most often compared. Rather, it's to the goddesses of platinum pop: Madonna, Britney, Christina, and Gwen—comparisons the singer finds a bit lazy. "Look, when I was a brunette, they called me Amy Winehouse. When I was a blonde, they called me Madonna. Then they called me Christina, then Gwen. I just don't think most people's reference points go back very far." While she does share a name with Gwen (Gaga's given name is Stefani Germanotta), while she once engaged in a bitchy back-and-forth in the press with Aguilera, and while she wrote a song for Spears ("Quicksand"), it's Madge who seems closest to the mark: both Italian-American girls who pulled themselves up by their bootstraps in the big, bad city, both are given to spectacle, both are sartorially adventurous and driven, and neither one apologizes for being pop.

All interesting, you might say, but will we be talking about Gaga in thirty years? That, of course, is a much bigger question. Decades-spanning superstars may well be a thing of the past. But those who predicted Gaga would be a one-and-done dance-pop footnote have already had to eat their words. And as for her being branded trashy? We've all heard that before. "I remember the cover of Madonna's 'Vogue' single and the lingerie and her hair—my mother was like, 'Ucch,'" laughs Gaga. "But I used to play it over and over." And now, all these years later, Queen Madge herself is attending Lady Gaga shows, or one last spring at least, at New York's Terminal 5. That night, as Gaga recalls, there was a show on and off stage. "My sister texted me and she was like, 'Madonna is 15 feet away from me. And there are two guys having sex in the audience. This is awesome!' I just remember thinking, Wow, this is exactly what I wanted. I've got Madonna and I've got gay sex!"

Gaga herself has copped to a certain degree of bisexuality, but says she never played it up because "I didn't want my gay fans to think I was using their community for edginess. You know, Ooh, she's edgy!" She considers her song "Future Love" to be in part an endorsement of same-sex marriage, and vows to never stop playing gay clubs, no matter how big things get. "With the exception of God, my family, and Matthew, and the Haus, and Vincent Herbert [who signed and discovered her], the gay community is the single reason that I am here today. I started out playing gay clubs in America, then I went to London to play G-A-Y, where I didn't think anyone knew who I was, and there were thousands of people there. How could I ever turn my back on those people who really fought for me? And besides the loyalty factor, playing in gay clubs is fun."

And yet, Gaga says what she does is not camp. "See, we don't see it that way. To us, it's just beautiful," she says. "The idea that Gaga is just kooky for the sake of being kooky is so wrong." Hmm, where would people get that impression? The cone-head hair she

sports on occasion? Or the stilettos-on-the-shoulders outfit she wore recently? Or the moment at this shoot when Gaga, lying on the floor in shimmering blue Balenciaga, hikes up the dress's hem far enough that the stylist feels the need to place down there a platinum blonde tuft that perfectly matches her hair? Tsk-tsk.

But say what you will—and plenty have—Gaga goes for it. Whether with a lightning bolt painted on her face, big bows in her hair, space-age cat suits, or that Chalayan-inspired bubble dress with matching piano, she can evoke David Bowie, Grace Jones, Björk, Stacey Q, Klaus Nomi, or Suzanne Bartsch. Throw in some Sprouse here and Margiela there and it's like hip fashion's greatest hits. Well, some might say mixaas, but what the checkout aisle arbiters of taste have to say won't keep Gaga up at night. "Us Weekly putting me on a worst-dressed list? I couldn't care less." On the other hand, she adds, "If Karl Lagerfeld called me an ugly hag, then I'd be upset. Because it's Karl Lagerfeld."

Whatever his opinion, Lagerfeld might want to stand back from Gaga's latest creation—the aforementioned fire bra unveiled in Toronto. As with most of her ideas, its execution fell on the shoulders of Matthew Williams, part tailor, part craftsman. He says of the bra, "It's really just sparklers—the old sparklers on the tits trick." But Gaga accuses him of modesty. "I called him from Hawaii and I was like, Matty, we need to make my tits blow up! And he made it happen.

No word yet on whether the bra will make an appearance on Gaga's upcoming fall tour with Kanye West, another artist fond of outsized shows that spare no expense. But she does admit that the two are "exploring aesthetics and new technology that neither of us have traveled, and we are attempting an epic story." Gaga talks a lot about her art, her work, the technology, the Haus, her creativity—and she knows it. "I'm sure to some people in the press it's like to a nauseating degree," she concedes. "There's Lady Gaga again, yakking about her art."

But all that yakking is just part of Gaga fighting the good fight. She insists time and again that pop is not lowbrow, dance music is not soulless, and that she is not playing a character but creating something with meaning. Her sincerity of purpose is admirable. Considering the well of blank R&B ciphers and Disney eunuchs into which 21st-century pop has thrown itself, maybe a performer who talks about creative vision, aspires to be avant-garde, counts among her circle of creative people designer Benjamin Cho and violinist Daniel Bernard Roumain, and sings the praises of drag queens—just maybe that's a good thing. Roll your eyes if you like—yes, maybe she ought to wear her heart and art a little less on her sleeve—but Gaga truly believes in all this.

For the day's final tableau, the Lady slips into a brown leather Fendi bustier and boots; her Haus of Gaga circuit-board glasses lend her a savage, vaguely Aztec look. Mario Testino snaps away—the woman with an album (and song) called The Fame and a single called "Paparazzi" shot by a fashion photographer known for his images of that ultimate victim of fame, Princess Diana. "Yes, Diana was the most iconic martyr of fame," says Gaga. "She died because of it." But Gaga adds—and this is no small point in a world of YouTube, Octomom, and Real Housewives—her album should not be seen as a glorification of celebrity. Rather it's about "the dream of wanting to make something of yourself," a dream that Gaga is undoubtedly realizing. "I took off those circuit-board glasses and looked at the computer monitor and I cried. I thought, We did that! We're doing something right!"

Lady Gaga is on tour with Kanye West in support of *The Fame* beginning October 11, 2009.

> "*US WEEKLY* PUTTING ME ON A WORST-DRESSED LIST?
> I COULDN'T CARE LESS. IF KARL LAGERFELD CALLED ME
> AN UGLY HAG, THEN I'D BE UPSET."
> —LADY GAGA

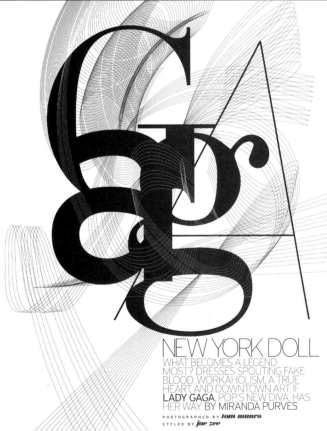

Blazer with tulle shoulder, **Viktor & Rolf**, price upon request, visit viktor-rolf .com. Suede elevated platform shoes, **Vivienne Westwood**, $640. *For details, see Shopping Guide.*

NEW YORK DOLL

WHAT BECOMES A LEGEND MOST? DRESSES SPOUTING FAKE BLOOD, WORKAHOLISM, A TRUE HEART, AND DOWNTOWN ART, IF **LADY GAGA**, POP'S NEW DIVA, HAS HER WAY. BY MIRANDA PURVES

PHOTOGRAPHED BY *tom munro*
STYLED BY *joe zee*

L'ITALO-AMERICANA
Padre mezzo palermitano,
madre di origini scandinave,
Lady Gaga è cresciuta a
Manhattan. È scema ciò
The Fame ha venduto
tre milioni di copie.

LADY GAGA

PERFETTA OPERAZIONE DI MARKETING O TALENTO PURO? SIAMO ANDATI A VEDERE COSA C'È DIETRO LA CANTANTE DEI RECORD. E ABBIAMO SCOPERTO CHE...
di ILARIA BELLANTONI foto di ELLEN VON UNWERTH/ART-COMMERCE/BLOG CG

MAX COVER STORY

T«Tenere i piedi per terra non è nel mio stile. Solo ora che sono completamente isolata nella mia scatola di follia posso davvero fare tutto quello che voglio. Per esempio, creare un mondo fantastico dove la gente viaggia senza passaporto. Oppure esibirmi su un palco con un bikini di porcellana e diventare la Barbie del giorno». Il che, nel caso di Lady Gaga, accade tutte le volte che esce di casa perché, per questa ventitreenne di New York, (s)vestirsi è una faccenda molto seria. «Una specie di performance artistica che non distrae affatto da quella musicale. Comunque, quando ho indossato il famoso mantello verde di Kermit la rana, con i ranocchi che mi coprivano le tette, l'ho fatto per protestare contro chi porta ancora le pellicce. Mica perché sono scema?
Questo non lo mette in dubbio nessuno.
Stefani Joanne Angelina Germanotta è un genio della comunicazione, oltre a un fenomeno da record: è la prima cantante in 17 anni da quando cioè esiste la classifica di Billboard, ad aver mandato al numero 1 quattro singoli di fila (Just dance, Poker Face, LoveGame e Paparazzi). Ace of Base, Avril Lavigne e Alanis Morissette si erano fermati a tre.
«All'inizio i discografici sostenevano che il mio cd non fosse abbastanza pop. È troppo elettronico... non funzionerà, si lamentavano. Io ero certa che fosse quanto di più nuovo la gente avesse mai

ascoltato». Tre milioni di persone le hanno dato ragione acquistando The Fame, che ha prodotto anche 20 milioni di download dei vari singoli. Così, nel giro di neanche un anno, la Interscope si è cosparsa il capo di cenere e ora pubblica The Fame Monster, versione deluxe del primo album con otto canzoni inedite (e perfino una sua ciocca di capelli in regalo).
«Ogni canzone rappresenta tutti i demoni che ho affrontato. Quando sono diventata famosa mi sono resa conto che avevo il terrore della morte, dell'alcol, delle droghe, della solitudine e della verità. Così ci ho scritto sopra un disco». Che ha pure un duetto con Beyoncé (Telephone) e Speechless, la ballata dedicata al padre: «Per 15 anni ha avuto problemi cardiaci, ma se n'è sempre fregato. Quel che sarà sarà, diceva. Quando ho scritto questo brano ero pronta a perderlo perché si stava sottoponendo a un'operazione a cuore aperto. Ora che hanno curato anche il suo cuore ricordatevi che la vita ci dà solo un set di genitori. Amateli».
Lady Gaga è una brava ragazza italo-americana con origini palermitane cresciuta a spaghetti all'olio e torte di mele. I suoi hanno fatto fortuna con Internet e, abitando nell'Upper West Side di Manhattan, l'hanno mandata al Convento del Sacro Cuore, la stessa scuola frequentata da Caroline Kennedy e Paris e Nicky Hilton. «Le suore
segue a pag. 58

BASSO PROFILO?
«La maggior parte del
tempo dimentico di essere
famosa. Mi riconoscono,
ma non frequento
ristoranti pretenziosi...

GAGA GODDESS
GRACE JONES

"I'm very inspired by Grace Jones. I've been watching all her videos. She's someone I'd love to work with."

PULL UP TO THE BUMPER BABY

Jamaican-born Grace Jones was a Warhol muse, a disco diva, and an extraordinary looking androgynous singer and model in the 1970s and '80s. After moving to New York in the mid-1960s, the almost six-foot daughter of a Pentecostal preacher attended a SUNY-sponsored community college (Onondaga) before trying to become a model. To make ends meet she became a shaven-headed go-go dancer and "discovered" herself in disco; she was, she has stated, a creature of the night. After failing to make it in the New York modeling world, Jones found her way to Paris, France. There she found modeling work and became a recognized face on the fashion and disco scene. She also became the protégé of photographer, designer, and illustrator Jean-Paul Goude. Although they never married, they had a child together, and Goude designed many of Jones' fantastic looks and art directed her 1980s record covers to dramatic effect.

In the mid-1970s Jones was signed to the Paris-based independent label Orfeo. Her first recording, an album titled *Portfolio*, was produced by disco wizard Tom Moulton and each side was made up of a continuous disco-beat driven medley of cover songs (which included Edith Piaf's "La Vie En Rose" and Stephen Sondheim's "Send in the Clowns"). A single taken from the album, "I Need a Man," made Number 1 on the U.S. dance charts via independent disco label Beam Junction in 1977. Her second album was titled *Fame* and, like the first, consisted of continuous disco-driven medleys. By the time of her third Moulton-produced disco medley album, *Muse*, Jones had been "discovered" and signed by the London-based record label owned by another Jamaican (albeit a rich, white man), Chris Blackwell.

Grace Jones' success as a disco diva took her back to New York, the center of the disco universe in the 1970s. She was an almost permanent fixture at the legendary Studio 54, where she became a constant Warhol companion.

Her height, prominent cheekbones, long legs, and aggressive poses soon created the rumor that "she" was a "he," a transsexual or transvestite. Jones' refusal to dress, act, or perform in the accepted lady-like manner of other models—she wore men's jackets over bikini bottoms with her hair cut severely short—made her an object of fascination for Warhol. Her first three album covers were drawn by Warhol's favorite *Interview* magazine cover illustrator, Richard Bernstein.

During the 1980s Jones became more successful as a pop singer, releasing a series of reggae-influenced electronic dance albums and singles, on many of which she'd speak-sing-rap the lyrics. Her videos and visual image, designed by Goude, had her wearing enormous square shoulderpads that offset her angular flat-top hair and sunglasses. Fashion magazines loved Jones, who was unpredictable and outrageous In 1981 and '82 she toured the world with her "One Man Show," which used the then-new video technology to project images behind her while she sang wearing magnificent costumes, masks, and a gorilla suit. It was the Monster Ball Tour of the 1980s!

Jones continues to record and release music.

Above: Grace Jones, still looking strong in 2010.

Opposite: Gaga in Teutonic mood during the Monster Ball concert, Radio City Music Hall, New York, January 2010.

AT LAST... THE FAME

AFTER attending online celeb-gossip columnist Perez Hilton's July Fourth bash in Las Vegas, and singing "Just Dance," Lady Gaga had some time off before flying out to appear on the televised Miss Universe 2008 contest in Vietnam. From there she made her way to Berlin for a fashion show before flying to Toronto and a radio station's summer party. During two weeks at the end of July and early August, Gaga prepared for the release of her debut album, *The Fame*.

The first edition of the album was officially released, on August 19, 2008, in Canada, which is why Gaga was in Niagara Falls. There she performed five songs from the album, ending with "Just Dance." The single was still making its way onto radio playlists and up the charts around the world, but the boost in promotion for the album would soon help it rise quickly to the top everywhere. After four dates in Canada, on August 22 Gaga was in San Francisco. There were numerous appearances on TV and radio in August, too—including MTV's TRL, as one of its last ever guests before closing.

The Fame was released as a CD and digital download in America on October 28, with a launch party titled The Fame Ball, at the Highline Ballroom in New York. For only $10 fans could meet and greet the Lady and get their CD signed, too.

The previous night Gaga had played Madison Square Garden with New Kids on the Block, and during the day she'd signed copies of *The Fame* in the Virgin Megastore at Union Square. Her old college was only a few blocks across town, but the life of a dreaming student must have seemed a million miles away—if she even thought about it at all. The success of *The Fame* would put even more distance between Gaga and Stefani Germanotta.

The Fame entered the *Billboard Hot 100* album charts at Number 17 in November 2008, but climbed steadily up the chart until March 2009 when it made Number 10. The album subsequently peaked at Number 2 in January 2010. It has sold over 600,000 digital downloads and more than three million CDs (and counting) in America. In February 2010 *The Fame* was classified as having sold over ten million copies worldwide.

Above: Fame came to both Gaga and *American Idol* runner-up David Archuleta in 2008.

"When I say to you,
there is nobody like me,
and there never was, that
is a statement I want
every woman to feel and
make about themselves.
I don't make it as a defense.
I make it as, OK, guys, it's
been two years, and I've
made a lot of music, and
I know my greatness is
individual. And I want
every woman to be able
to say that."

POKER FACE

"**M**u-mu-mu-ma, muu-mu-mu-mah . . ." Proving that she's a winner, Lady Gaga's second single taken from *The Fame*, "Poker Face," was released in Australia during late September 2008. She was touring there at the time and it entered the charts at 26 but reached the top slot a few weeks later. America had to wait until almost Christmas before getting the single release. Maybe because of the time of year it went in at 92, and took until March 2009 to reach the Number 3 slot. Following a nation-wide broadcast appearance on the *American Idol* TV show in April 2009, "Poker Face" became her second (and consecutive) Number 1 hit single. "Just Dance" had reached the top spot in mid-January 2009.

The bpm of "Poker Face" are not quite as rapid as those on "Just Dance," but it's still a dance number. The chanted, deep-voice hook that opens the song, "Mu-mu-mu-ma, muu-mu-mu-mah" sounded familiar to fans of an earlier Eurodisco sound, who claimed it was a sample from German disco act Boney M's "Ma Baker." The backing vocal sound on the song also bears a resemblance to Boney M. But they were not the elements of the song that captured everyone's attention, however.

The song contains a line which rhymes "bluffin" with "muffin," and was clearly sexual. Or so interviewers kept insisting. When asked, Gaga said, "I took that line from another song I wrote but never released, called 'Blueberry Kisses.' It was about a girl singing to her boyfriend about how she wants him to go down on her, and I used the lyric. [*Sings*] 'Blueberry

Below: Gaga wields her disco stick in Sydney, Australia, September 2008.

Following page: Gaga in Malta, June 2008.

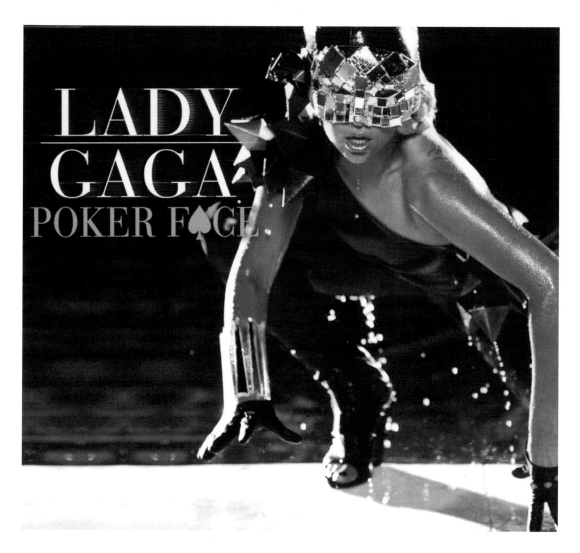

LADY
GAGA
POKER FACE

kisses, the muffin man misses them kisses.'" Subsequently the lines with muffin in them have been "beeped" out by some broadcasters, as have lines about Russian roulette and the word "gun." It only added to Gaga's notoriety, of course, and prompted growing interest in her and her music.

The song mixes gambling and sexual imagery, so the video naturally plays with both subjects. By giving them a major product placement in the video, bwin.com allowed the shoot to take place at their Poker Island site on Ibiza, a Spanish island in the Mediterranean. Gaga wears a mirrored face mask and black off-the-shoulder PVC catsuit as she emerges from a swimming pool between her two Great Danes (mother and son, named Lava and Rumpus). She also wears her "pop culture" sunglasses in the video, which includes a strip poker session that becomes a dancing "orgy," and a Gaga "hair bow."

By relentlessly promoting both her debut album release and that of "Poker Face," Gaga seemed to be everywhere you looked, in different countries on separate continents in late 2008. At the tail end of the year she was in Europe, performing in the Scandinavian countries. In the run-up to Christmas she was to be heard in interviews on radio stations across America. Her support tour with New Kids on the Block ended on December 4. The video for "Poker Face" was made in late October 2008. She hadn't stopped working for pretty much the whole year. As the New Year began it didn't look as if things were set to change much.

Her diary for the first three months of 2009 included videoshoots, trips to Europe, more U.S. promotion, and live performances. Perhaps most thrillingly, however, it included chart watches around the world as *The Fame* and "Poker Face" began their assault on charts of every nation.

"I love Boney M, so perhaps subconsciously it came out in the song."

5
FAME

In January 2009 Lady Gaga had been a resident of Los Angeles for twelve months, although she'd spent probably less than half of that time on the West Coast. Her touring and promotional schedule during 2008 had taken her around the world. Yet her career was only just beginning, and she was set to make many more long-distance trips in order to build on the work already done.

In the fourth quarter of 2008 Gaga had toured the arenas of America as support act to New Kids on the Block. Her first appearance was at the Staples Center in L.A. on October 8, and her last at the Monterrey Arena on December 4. She'd also managed to slot in PAs at clubs after the NKOTB shows in most cities they played at—often gay clubs and hip nightspots. Gaga was proving to be a very hard worker, and her ability to perform at the highest level in front of both big crowds and intimate audiences stood her in good stead for the promotional push of 2009 that would make her a truly international superstar.

With an album to promote as well as not one, but two, hit singles—both "Just Dance" and "Poker Face" were sharing chart space in countries around the world—Gaga's name was everywhere. Soon her ever-changing public image would be everywhere, too. By the simple fact of appearing dressed in exciting, witty, and inventive outfits, Lady Gaga gathered acres of print and online coverage from the world's media. She looked, acted, and talked like an old-fashioned star of the distant past—kind of like Marilyn Monroe channeled through Madonna and reinvented by Gaga. Lady Gaga exuded glamour, opulence, elegance, and an exotic sex appeal in a way that no star of either stage, screen, or radio had done for well over a decade.

In 2009 Gaga became the living embodiment of *The Fame*.

Opposite: Grrr! In Mannheim, Germany, August 2008.

WORLD DOMINATION

Although Lady Gaga's year began in America, with an appearance on NBC's *Tonight Show with Jay Leno* on January 8, she had to leave the country almost immediately after it and travel to the United Kingdom. Once there, she began a stint as the opening act on the Pussycat Dolls' World Domination Tour for the European and Australian dates.

After a warm-up appearance at London's biggest gay club, Heaven, the previous night, Gaga took to the AECC stage in Aberdeen, Scotland, on January 18 at 8 p.m. While the gig was billed as the Pussycat Dolls' night, there were enough fans screaming for Gaga to make it seem like it was at least a co-headline tour.

Gaga was a smash hit success and as the arena tour exploded through the UK and Ireland, she was reviewed favorably by almost everyone. She was invited onto several UK TV shows where she would perform and chat. Every appearance saw a different Gaga outfit make its debut which would guarantee a mass of photographs in the next day's media of Gaga. Interestingly, while many of Gaga's outfits revealed an expanse of flesh, none of them gave the impression of being overtly sexual or provocative in any traditionally sensual way. While the Domination headline act strutted onstage in clichéd stripper stockings, garterbelts, and corset outfits—they were after all originally burlesque dancers (apart from Nicole) who'd appeared in a soft porno magazine—Gaga's outfits were more surreal, science-fiction inspired creations.

It didn't go without notice that the cover art for "Just Dance," "Poker Face," and *The Fame* did not depict a semi-naked or sexually explicit photo of Lady Gaga. That would be just too easy, too expected. Gaga wanted to do the unexpected, always.

While she was in the UK, "Just Dance" made Lady Gaga the top popstar in America when it reached Number 1 on the *Billboard* charts at last. *The Fame*, having entered the UK album charts at Number 3, hung around the upper reaches of the chart for the whole of Gaga's stay in the country (and finally made the Number 1 spot in April 2009). On the day of the UK release of *The Fame*, January 12, it was announced via her MySpace site that Lady Gaga would be undertaking her debut American headline tour, beginning on March 12, 2009 in California. To be titled The Fame Ball Tour, it would include stage sets, costumes, a band, dancers, and just about anything that the Haus of Gaga could come up with by the time Gaga stepped out on stage at the House of Blues in San Diego.

In late February Gaga had appeared on the top music awards show in the UK, the BRIT Awards, where she sang a duet with the Pet Shop Boys and Killers' singer Brandon Flowers. It was the performance of a star, a headline act, someone that the long-established electro-pop geniuses of the Pet Shop Boys would gladly be seen and heard with.

When the European leg of the Pussycat Dolls tour finished the day after the BRITs in Berlin, Germany, Gaga took a few days in Paris and Madrid before heading back to L.A. and rehearsals. She was determined that her first North American tour proper—not just singing to backing tracks in clubs, but at renowned live music venues—was going to be something well worth seeing.

Opposite: With the Pet Shop Boys at the BRIT Awards, London, February 2009.

"My album covers are not sexual at all, which was an issue at my record label. I fought for months, and I cried at meetings. They didn't think the photos were commercial enough . . . The last thing a young woman needs is another picture of a sexy pop star writhing in sand, covered in grease, touching herself."

"I think there are different kinds of fame. There's fame which is plastic and about paparazzi and money and being rich, and then there's the fame, which is when no one knows who you are but everyone wants to know who you are. That's what The Fame is about—for everybody on the planet to stop being either jealous or obsessive about what they don't have and start acting like they do. It's about carrying yourself like you've got it all."

GAGA GODDESS
DALE BOZZIO

DESTINATION UNKNOWN

In one of her regular tweet updates written from New Zealand in March 2010, Gaga wrote of the previous evening's show at the Vector Arena in Auckland that, "I swear tonight didn't feel like an arena. It felt like 15,000 sweaty kids in a club in 1985." There is little higher praise that Gaga can give than to evoke the spirit of that time before her birth when clubbing meant dressing up, and when getting ready was as important as arriving and being seen.

At the beginning of the 1980s a "new wave" of clubbers began to form bands as much to impress with the way they dressed as with their music. In the UK the New Romantic scene gave the world Duran Duran, Spandau Ballet, and A Flock of Seagulls. In New York the New Wave that had emerged in the previous decade from CBGBs with Patti Smith, the Ramones, and Blondie leading the way hit the west coast and morphed into a far more elegantly attired wave led by glamorous synth-rock and power-pop bands. Among them were the all-female Go-Gos and Bangles, the synth-rock Motels and Missing Persons. The all-inclusive nature of the New Wave, in which women were considered as capable of being musicians as men, meant that a generation of young women had decided to start bands, and became successful because of their musical skills as much as for their looks.

Dale Bozzio was one of them. Although originally from Boston, Bozzio (formerly Consalvi) formed the band Missing Persons with her husband Terry Bozzio and guitarist Warren Cuccurullo in 1980. The three had met in L.A. when Dale had sung on Frank Zappa's weirdo jazz-rock opera *Joe's Garage* of 1979. A former *Playboy* bunny and model, as a performer Dale showed a flair for constructing theatrical costumes, which, with her extravagantly dyed hair and a unique, "squeaky" style of singing, added to the band's appeal. After two years spent becoming local musical legends (with their wild live performances during which Dale would appear onstage in self-constructed outfits that included a bikini top made of silver foil or with her breasts covered only by black tape), the band signed with a major record label. Her outfits improved to the extent that she wore

a tiny bikini top made of gold material and skin-tight silver lurex pants with six-inch stiletto heels for an appearance at the televised live U.S. Festival in 1983. At other times Dale wore clear-plastic skirts and tops, multi-colored hair, big sunglasses, and a mirrored panel as a skirt with a mirrored bra-top and posed as a plastic mannequin for the cover of the single sleeve to "Destination Unknown" (as well as in the video for another single, "Words").

The Missing Persons debut album, *Spring Session M*, was released in 1982 and went on to earn a gold record. The two singles taken from it—"Destination Unknown" and "Words"—became Top 50 *Billboard* hits, and Top 10 radio hits in California and New York. The romantic, elaborate video for "Destination Unknown" received heavy MTV play, and rightly so. In it Dale appears in a variety of Princess-style dresses, with a piece of jagged mirror stuck on her cheek, her hair a mass of white-blonde frizz highlighted by a strong pink streak.

After four years of only modest success, Missing Persons disbanded (and the Bozzio marriage collapsed). Dale signed a solo contract with Prince's Paisley Park label. She released one album, *Riot in English*, in 1988. A single with accompanying sexy video featuring her in leather with bondage straps, spikes, and stockings, titled "Simon Simon," was a dance hit in 1988. Dale never made it really big, but the influence of her wild outfits and attitude can be seen in some of Gaga's outfits.

Opposite: Valentine's Day 2009 and Gaga is hard at work as usual, this time on stage in Munich, Germany.

Below: The cover for the Missing Persons single "Destination Unknown" from 1982, with Dale modelling a plexiglass bikini.

FAME
BALL
TOUR

WHEN Lady Gaga's debut headline tour was announced, she conjured up the spirit of Andy Warhol in telling people to expect not just a pop music tour, but more of a "concept," which would include performance, multimedia, art, and fashion. On MTV in advance of the dates Gaga said, "It's not really a tour, it's more of a traveling party." She went on to explain how she wanted to take her audience back in time. "It's going to be as if you're walking into New York circa 1974." Regardless of the fact that a visit to New York in 1974 was far from a pleasant or risk-free experience, it's the idea Gaga has of that time and place that she hoped to create at her Fame Ball. It would be more about attitude than exactitude.

Gaga explained the show would contain "an art installation in the lobby, a DJ spinning your favorite records in the main room, and then the most haunting performance that you've ever seen on stage." Does that sound like she is boasting? If so, then it's forgivable, surely? She's simply insistent on giving her fans the best show possible and is aware that they have as much to contribute to the night's success as she has. As the tour sold out within hours of tickets going on sale, and as many places as possible fit in second shows, Gaga realized that she had a small army of fans, and they would—as the army grew and grew—become more important to her and would be addressed by her from the stage, TV, and radio. The fast-selling tickets and huge success of her music releases must have made her feel that she was doing something right, too.

The Fame Ball was a multimedia presentation. Before the opening date on March 11 at a *Star* magazine birthday party in L.A., Gaga and her old friend Lady Starlight made some movies. In order for the show to continue while Gaga had to be offstage getting changed, a large screen covering the stage showed three short films in which Gaga plays a character named Candy Warhol. Titled *The Heart*, *The Brain*, and *The Face*, they show "Candy" getting ready for a show and segue neatly into the appearance on stage of Gaga in spectacular outfits.

The first outfit was black, cut in a geometric shape with reflective triangles forming an over-skirt. After three numbers the second film (*The Brain*) showed "Candy" doing her hair. Gaga reappeared in a white leotard with Bowie-esque lightning flashes, and during the next two numbers she rode a small motorscooter around the stage and put on a domino-covered hat. After a brief jam with Space Cowboy and the band, Gaga departed the stage while they carried on playing. When she returned the Lady appeared in a bubble dress seated at a perspex piano. After two numbers another film showed (*The Face*, in which Candy learns to talk), while Gaga changed costumes. She reappeared wearing a tutu and enormous pointed shoulder pads. She put on her LED "sunglasses," which flash the message "pop music will never be low brow," and waved her disco stick around as the show finished on a real high. After another short session from Space Cowboy, Gaga returned for an encore wearing a nude corset, naval cap, and fingerless gloves with Gaga spelled out in diamanté on both. The gig ended amid a sea of balloons and confetti, with sold-out audiences crying for even more.

The Fame Ball received nothing but rave reviews wherever it played—and it played everywhere, crisscrossing America, Europe, the Middle East, the Far East (including China), and Australasia. In all, the Fame Ball took place more than seventy times between March and the end of September.

Opposite: Gaga on the Fame Ball Tour, Irvine, California, May 2009.

"The Fame Ball is so perfectly an avant-garde-performance-art-fashion installation, put in a blender and vomited out as a pop show . . . it's the ultimate creative orgasm for me—no limitations, I'm free."

GAGA GOD
ALEXANDER MCQUEEN

"Thank you to Lee McQueen."

MORE IS MORE

Lady Gaga first publicly name-checked British designer Alexander McQueen in 2007 during a song co-written with RedOne, titled "Fashion." Although it was first recorded by "star" of MTV's reality show *The Hills*, Heidi Montag, and released by her in June 2008, it was Gaga's version that made it onto an episode of *Ugly Betty* and then on to the soundtrack of the movie *Confessions of a Shopaholic*. Of all the large number of cutting edge fashion designers mentioned in "Fashion"—including Jimmy Choo, Dolce & Gabbana, Prada, and Vivienne Westwood—none are quite as edgy, surreal or outrageous as McQueen was; even if Westwood had her moments.

A four-time winner of the prestigious British Designer of the Year Award (1996, 1997, 2001, and 2003) Alexander "Lee" McQueen (1969–2010) began his career in fashion in the most conventional way. He started as a trainee to a traditional Savile Row tailor, learning how to measure, handle, and cut cloth. The skills learned on Savile Row helped him to get into art school (he earned no high school qualifications, leaving at age sixteen), where, via his Master's graduation show three years later, he came to the notice of the noted and influential London-based fashionista Isabella Blow (muse to master milliner Philip Treacy, another Gaga fave and the man who created her blue, 1920s-style telephone hat). Blow helped introduce McQueen to the inner circles of London's fashion world where he soon thrived. He directed one of Icelandic singer Bjork's videos, and in return she appeared in one of his designs on the cover of her *Homogenic* album in 1997.

McQueen had spent some time in the early 1990s attending performances and shows put on by Leigh Bowery (see page 83), and appreciated the shock power of fashion. In a 1996 show he had models wear bumster jeans that showed a large part of their rear cleavage; slightly less severely cut versions soon flooded the market. He put human skull motifs on materials, and scarves bearing his design became almost de

rigueur wear for rock stars and actors. His fashion shows became spectacles at which everyone wanted to be seen. For one show he had models appear as versions of Spanish galleon ships and staged a "shipwreck" on the catwalk.

Gaga was naturally drawn to McQueen's lovingly produced and extravagant work. She featured a pair of his fabulous lobster claw diamante platform shoes in the video for "Bad Romance," for instance. Inspired by Leigh Bowery, the seemingly impossible-to-wear shoes are proven by Gaga to be practical as well as beautiful as she struts in them on screen.

The lobster shoes were not the only Bowery-inspired touch to be found in McQueen's work, and the two men also shared some similarities in terms of their upbringing. Both were physically large men, from non-traditional fashion backgrounds. McQueen's lack of formal education would have been a huge disadvantage had he not come to the fore in the wake of Bowery and Westwood's influence on the London fashion scene. Like Bowery, McQueen was openly gay and grew up in a time and environment when that was not easy for his working-class family to accept. "I'm the pink sheep of the family," he had joked, later changing the color to gold when he was rich and famous.

Both McQueen and Bowery grew up close to their mothers, and those bonds didn't lessen for McQueen, it seems. Lee was the last of six children born to Joyce McQueen. She was a schoolteacher and supported him in his dreams of becoming a fashion designer, which he claimed he'd known about the same time that he knew he was gay—at age six—when no one else did. When Joyce died on February 2, 2010, a big part of Lee's life force went with her. Unable to bear her loss he sadly took his own life on February 11, the day before her funeral was to take place. Five days later Gaga performed at the BRIT Awards show in a McQueen-inspired huge wig, white embroidered face mask, and body stocking. Collecting the first of three awards she thanked her friend, Lee McQueen.

Opposite (top): Alexander McQueen receives applause at the end of his ready-to-wear 2003 spring-summer collection in Paris, October 2002. Isabella Blow can be seen in the front row, wearing a blue hat.

Opposite (bottom): The 2010 BRIT Awards in London came just after McQueen's death in February. Gaga dedicated her performance to him.

LOVEGAME

IN the middle of the Fame Ball Tour, Lady Gaga let everyone know exactly what a "disco stick" was when the single version of "LoveGame" was released in April, 2009. It was a natural choice for the third single to be taken from *The Fame*, since it was written in the studio with RedOne in a burst of inspiration in January along with "Just Dance" and "Poker Face," and so has a similar, almost familiar, feel and sound about it.

With its 100+ bpm, robotic refrain, and synthesizer beat, "LoveGame" already sounds like classic Gaga Eurodisco for the twenty-first century. But where the previous two Gaga singles implied a sexual content, "LoveGame" is far more explicit. The Lady keeps asking for a ride on someone's "disco stick," and while it's possible to interpret the request as being made to persons of either sex, the lyrics have a strictly heterosexual content. This story, Gaga says, is as old as time and involves a male, a female and a "huh." That "huh" being the disco stick for which another, cruder name was implied earlier in the song in a rhyme with the word "block."

The single's video, shot in L.A. and first seen in Australia and the UK in February of 2009 (where it had been released earlier than in America), is set in New York. Accessing a subway setting via a manhole cover embossed with Haus of Gaga, the camera swoops to find the Lady naked but for purple body paint and glitter, singing between two men as they sit astride a short bench in what looks like a locker room. The scene cuts to Gaga in a chainmail headdress and white bodysuit, brandishing her disco stick (which lights up), dancing amid a bunch of very camp, leather-, jeans- and chain-bedecked male dancers. Later in the video she is wearing a short, white biker jacket over

the bodysuit and then a pair of silver-studded bikini bottoms over pantyhose with a black leather jacket. The dance scenes, which move to a subway train and parking lot, are intercut with shots of Gaga naked but for the paint and glitter. The video includes a lot of Michael Jackson–inspired crotch grabbing and fist pumping just like in his video for "Bad." There are also shots of Gaga in a police-style black leather cap with chainmail visor, and we see her first on-screen lesbian kiss, with a parking lot attendant in a steamed-up booth.

It's a fun video, and director Joseph Khan (best known for his videos of Britney's "Toxic" and Eminem's "Without Me") does a good job. But it's not up to the standards of the then still

"I was at a nightclub, and I had quite a sexual crush on somebody, and I said to them, 'I wanna ride on your disco stick.' The next day, I was in the studio, and I wrote the song in about four minutes. When I play the song live, I have an actual stick—it looks like a giant rock-candy pleasuring tool—that lights up."

to be seen "Paparazzi" video, which had been shot three months after this, and with a vastly increased budget.

The single didn't sell well at first, debuting at Number 96 on the *Billboard* charts in its first week and then falling out of the charts until, six weeks and over 100,000 digital downloads later, it hit Number 5. That was the first indication that Gaga is a uniquely twenty-first-century pop star. For the first time a pop artist became a major international star on the sales of digital downloads and not physical product.

Kids downloaded Gaga singles; the majority of her fans didn't walk into stores and buy CDs—although a fair few hundred thousand have done that since. Her fans would leave home to see her, but they would stay home to buy her music.

Below: Trying on hats in the Gift Lounge at the MuchMusic HQ, June 2009, Toronto.

SUMMER FUN
IN THE SUN

THE Fame Ball Tour was a global sell-out success. From America, and after completing her duty to open for the Pussycat Dolls in New Zealand and Australia in May 2009, Gaga took her Fame Ball to Japan, Singapore, and Korea. Legions of new fans joined the already converted Gaga devotees in the Far East, prompting the booking of a return visit for the Fame Ball in August. After a single date in Canada on June 19, Gaga and crew headed for Europe again. On July 4 and 5, Gaga opened for the recently re-formed British boy band Take That's Circus Live at the largest venue in England, London's Wembley Stadium (capacity 70,000+). The Fame Ball was then staged in Malta, France, Scotland, and Ireland before playing at England's largest indoor arena, the O2 (capacity 20,000+), on July 14.

From the O2 Gaga went on to invade and capture the hearts, minds, and dancing feet of legions of fans in Germany, the Netherlands, Switzerland, Austria, Spain, Finland, Norway, Denmark, and Sweden before heading East to Japan, Korea, the Philippines, Singapore, and China. She then made a stop-off in Israel on the way back to England and America for the final two shows.

In England Gaga revisited a bit of what must have felt like her distant past, when she appeared at three open-air music festivals, including the prestigious Glastonbury Festival. As with the Lollapalooza festival, at which she and Lady Starlight had performed in 2007, Glastonbury had the reputation of being able to make or break an act in the UK, but usually an act that made it big there played indie or "serious" rock music. Not many pop acts with huge cross-generational appeal such as Gaga were asked to appear. Aware of the musical snobbery that surrounds the event, Gaga decided to put on a decidedly adult, X-rated performance for Glastonbury, and hope that both the quality of her music and the art shock of her performance would serve her well.

For some bizarre reason, rumors had begun to circulate on anti-Gaga websites that she was actually a "he." Gaga had played with the idea of ambiguity since her time with Lady Starlight, Breedlove, and Anna Copacabana on the Lower East Side. However hard it is to think of Gaga as anything but a woman, since she simply doesn't have a boyish figure, the rumors would not go away. Determined to have some fun with the idea, after two songs Gaga left the stage for a costume change. Reappearing on-stage on her red motorscooter, wearing a short, tight red dress with studs over the shoulder, she'd put a fake penis inside her bikini pants. Stepping off the scooter, the crowd and particularly the photographers at the stage front got a quick flash of a flesh-colored protuberance "peeking" out of her pants. Making no reference to the joke Gaga went into "Boys Boys Boys" and the show continued to rock the appropriately named Other Stage.

Lady Gaga's show at Glastonbury not only sparked a ridiculous new rumor that she was a hermaphrodite, which lead to her posing for UK music magazine *Q* with a large fake penis inside her pants, but also earned her enormous respect from music mags and newspapers. Broadsheet and serious newspaper the *Guardian* wrote of her set, "Pop madness/brilliance from a performer at home in front of the huge crowds." Gaga's exploding bra, which spit sparks from Madonna-like conical cups, earned a lot of coverage, with the normally unshockable indie mag *NME* headlining their review "Lady Gaga spits fire from her breasts at Glastonbury." The review majored on her outfits, which also included a mirrored gladiator-style skirt with matching breastplate and a bubble dress. The stuffy BBC refused to broadcast her appearance live, despite listing the time for it, and chose instead to show "highlights"—which didn't include the exploding bra version of "Eh, Eh."

Gaga proved at Glastonbury that she was a truly modern pop music creation, able to shock and entertain, able to make people think as well as look and listen. She had everyone in the UK talking about her, and the photographs and video clips from the show soon had millions of hits on public access websites from people around the world.

"I used to go to festivals, get naked, and take acid."

GAGA GOD
THE DISCO BALL

"Favorite elements to my shows—the disco balls, hot pants, sequins, and stilettos . . ."

SPIN ME ROUND

It has many names and obscure beginnings. It exists in pretty much every place where people meet to dance, sing, have fun, and party, and has inspired many inventions by the Haus of Gaga. The disco ball—or mirror ball, or glitter ball—is a simple spherical object covered in tiny flat mirrors, usually suspended from the ceiling and able to revolve slowly. Light is directed at the ball and the resultant reflective patterns move around the room, dazzling onlookers, conjuring an atmosphere that now inevitably suggests flared trousers, platform sole shoes, a man in a white suit, and the sound of falsetto-voiced men singing, "ha-ha-ha-ha stayin' alive."

The disco movement which emerged at the end of the 1960s spread across America like a funky dancing disease. It negated divisions in American society in a way that civil rights marchers could only dream about, and had burly hetero macho-men dressing in silk and see-through shirts, thick soles, jewelry, and expensively coiffured hair. Bored with protesting and fighting a losing war in Vietnam, America took to the dance floor in order to forget all their troubles.

Not that the disco movement was devoid of politics. The Gay Rights movement wiggled its hips and emerged from the Stonewall Inn in Greenwich Village one steamy night in 1969. Elegantly attired drag queens, fed up with being harassed all the time while they tried to drink and dance in peace, revolted against a raid and began throwing bottles and stones at the police. Within weeks the Village had various well-organized and militant Gay Rights committees established. A year later the first annual Gay Rights march took place in New York, with similar events staged in L.A., San Francisco, and Chicago. The marchers wore hot pants, feather boas, drag outfits, and blew whistles as they danced through the streets.

As one memorable scene in the movie *Saturday Night Fever* shows, for the whole disco generation that is represented by Tony Manero, dressing up to go out was almost as big a part of the night as was the dancing. It's little wonder that Gaga has used the disco ball so often on stage and in her videos; it's a universally recognized symbol of a good night out.

Gaga has regularly used a disco ball in making her outfits. She has designed and worn mirrored masks, hats, skirts, shoulder pads, and hats. There is a Gaga mirrored keyboard worn like a guitar via a shoulderstrap, and she has talked about having a mirrored grand piano.

The disco ball and the spirit of disco, particularly that of dressing up as if performing a show every night and always looking your best, is pure Gaga. While she is an entertainer and her mission is to put on a show—and none were as spectacular as her appearance at the MTV video awards in September 2009, covered in fake blood and ending with her being "hung" from the ceiling—she believes that her every moment should be spent looking like a star. It's a continuation of her Warhol-inspired Fame philosophy. No one should want to see a true star dressed like a "normal" person, she says. A star should be untouchable, always reflected in the bright lights of a shining mirror ball.

Opposite: Mirroring the disco ball on stage at Nokia Theatre L.A., December 2009.

Below: Gaga in communion with her disco ball at a magazine event in March 2008, South Beach, Florida.

WELCOME TO PEREZ

By the end of the Fame Ball Tour in September 2009, Gaga was to be seen everywhere. In magazines, on TV, radio stations, and YouTube, Gaga performances, videos, and interviews proliferated. America was taking notice, and it wasn't just the public who saw her as a good thing. She had made some good and powerful friends while touring and appearing around the world. One of the most influential of her showbusiness pals is Miami-born gossip blogger and television host Perez Hilton.

A drama graduate of NYU (2000), Hilton moved to L.A. and attempted to build a career as an actor, which never took off. Before moving west, Hilton had spent some time working in PR for gay rights organization Gay and Lesbian Alliance Against Defamation (GLAAD), and as a writer and then editor for a gay men's magazine. In 2005 Hilton, still using his real name of Mario LaVandeira and living in L.A., began a celebrity gossip blog titled pagesixsixsix.com (666 being the Biblical "sign of the beast"). On it he wrote about time spent at parties, launches, and events with members of L.A. celebrity hierarchy. However, after NYP Holdings Inc., who'd already registered the site name, sued him, Mario became Perez Hilton and a legend began. NYP Holdings withdrew its complaint against him two months later, but by then perezhilton.com had established itself as the country's premier fun celeb gossip site. A year later Hollywood rival gossip site TheInsider.com (owned by TV corp CBS) had helped put Perez on the international map by naming his site "Hollywood's Most Hated."

The Hilton trademark became his use of celeb photos, on which he hand-scrawls comments, and low-tech design sensibility. The site

Left: Perez Hilton in affectionate homage to his superstar chum.

looked (and continues to look) as if it's run out of his spare bedroom—which it was, originally. Visitors to the site can believe that they've stumbled upon an amateur work of love. Yet in 2007—before it became even bigger than it is now—Hilton charged $16,000 a week for a banner ad. Perez—whose support on his site for old friend Paris Hilton was undaunted by criticism of either of them—proved his worth to developing music acts in 2007 when he actively promoted the debut album by Mika. In the two weeks following Hilton's promotion, *Life in Cartoon Motion* sold 50,000 copies, more than twice as many as it had previously. Mika's support of gay rights and supposed homosexuality

"Perez Hilton is brilliant to me. Because he's taken something that people don't think is valid, don't think is important, and he's made them obsessed with it. People are obsessed with him. They're obsessed with his site, they're obsessed with what he does."

appealed to Perez in much the same way that Gaga's has. While he had difficult public relations with Britney Spears—whose public fall from grace he relished reporting—she asked him to record a video intro for her Circus Tour (he agreed). Madonna has publicly dedicated live song performances to him.

Perez gained a reputation for being bitchy about stars and for "outing" celebrities who had not, prior to his intervention, revealed their supposed sexual preferences. Among them were former American Idol contestant Clay Aiken, 'N Sync member Lance Bass, and former *Doogie Howser M.D.* star Neil Patrick Harris. For Perez Hilton, Gaga's strong pro-gay rights stand made her a true artist, an outstanding human being, and a near-bosom pal. His fascination with fame and what it means also chimes with Lady Gaga. It's little wonder they're buddies and tweet each other when they can't meet in person.

Above: Perez Hilton and Gaga at the MOCA NEW 30th anniversary gala, November 2009, Los Angeles.

"I find that men get away with saying a lot in this business, and that women get away with saying very little . . . In my opinion, women need and want someone to look up to that they feel has the full sense of who they are, and says, 'I'm great.'"

THE FAME MONSTER

WHILE Gaga was touring, she was also writing and recording a new album. Wherever she was in the world, she would go into studios to work on new material, sometimes with members of her band—guitarist Nic Constantine, bassist Tom Kafafian, drummer Andy Brobjer, and keyboard player Brian London—but often it would be her, a studio crew and RedOne, who'd fly in specially for Gaga.

Naturally, given how the new songs had been written, the subject of them was fame, although now it was a different kind of fame. The second album was about the monster that fame had become to Gaga. As she explained it, "I find *The Fame Monster* to be completely different than *The Fame*. I've evolved, but artists should evolve. In the '70s and the '60s, artists evolved all the time—from album to album the music was changing, the feeling was changing, the artists seemed almost entirely different than who they were five or six years before." Given that it had hardly been nine months since *The Fame* had been finished, the change wouldn't be drastic.

The eight tracks making up the *Monster* collection, brilliant as they are, were not considered sufficient to release as an album. Originally, Gaga disagreed about a plan to re-release *The Fame* with an extra EP of new songs. The compromise was the release of an almost bewildering array of different versions, for different territories, and in America too. While there was a single CD edition of *Monster*, the new recordings were also packaged with *The Fame* as a two-disc album and released with the title *The Fame Monster*.

For the truly devoted—and wealthy—Gaga fans there was a Deluxe boxed set edition of both albums, with a lock of hair from a wig, a

jigsaw puzzle, posters, 3D glasses, fanzines, a book of photos, and a note from Gaga.

Gaga embarked upon another trans-North American tour, The Monster Ball, on November 27 in Canada. Three weeks into it she made a brief detour to the UK to perform "Speechless" at the Royal Variety Performance, at which Her Majesty Queen Elizabeth II was present. In a witty reminder of the Beatles' performance at the same event in 1963, Gaga said, "Good evening Blackpool, let me hear you rattle your jewelry." John Lennon had quipped, "Will people in the cheaper seats clap your hands, and the rest of you rattle your jewelry."

Opposite: Gaga in a Schiaparelli-inspired creation, onstage at the American Music Awards 2009, Los Angeles.

"It's been a life-changing year for me creatively as a musician and a performance artist. I walk away from the Fame Ball humbled by my little monsters—my fans—and proud of the Haus for all its successes amidst the adversity of the industry."

PAPARAZZI

"IT's the first interesting 'pop' record that I wrote," Lady Gaga said of this, the fourth single to become a hit taken from *The Fame*. "The song is about a few different things," she continued, "It's about my struggles; do I want fame or do I want love? It's also about wooing the paparazzi to fall in love with me. It's about the media whoring, if you will, watching ersatzes make fools of themselves. It's a love song for the cameras, but it's also a love song about fame or love—can you have both, or can you only have one?"

At the time Gaga was living the dichotomy. She had found worldwide fame, as well as an enormous amount of love—from her fans. Of course she had family love in spades, but there was no single one person who was her special lover. But how could there be when millions of people loved her, almost, it seemed, unconditionally? That they did was partly because her image was everywhere of course, constantly captured by the world's press photographers, the paparazzi.

It wasn't always easy for Gaga, being constantly watched and filmed, as she also explained when asked about the single. "I just thought that it was turning into a constant problem, so what's [a] more important thing to write about than the absolute hugest part of media culture? The paparazzi." From her point of view in front of the camera, Gaga could see the effect on those people who sat in front of the image taken. For a brief time when the single came out Gaga carried her own camera and turned it on the photographers as they snapped away at her (Warhol had carried a camera with him in the 1970s and '80s to do the same).

On release in late September the single made the lower reaches of the *Billboard* singles chart and slowly worked its way into the Top 10. Having been released early in the year in the UK and Europe, it had already been a hit there. "Paparazzi" was aided in its sales by the

eight-minute video, directed by Swede Jonas Akerlund. A mini-movie, it features Gaga in a variety of great costumes (including a replica of an outfit worn by a robot in the 1929 silent movie *Metropolis*) and, after recovering from a fall from a balcony, taking revenge on her boyfriend who'd pushed her off the balcony, by poisoning him. It looks sumptuous, and Gaga is stunning.

It takes a few viewings before the storyline of "Paparazzi" becomes clear, but that was part of the plan, as Gaga revealed later: "I thought about performance art and shock art and how Paris Hilton and her sister and Lindsay Lohan and Nicole Richie are shock artists in their own way. They're not necessarily doing fine arts—something they put in the museums—but it's an art form."

With the video for "Paparazzi" Gaga made wonderful art in a commercial way that Warhol would have loved.

Opposite: Gaga snapped by the subject of her song, London, January 2009.

"I just thought that it was turning into a constant problem, so what's [a] more important thing to write about than the absolute hugest part of media culture? The paparazzi. It's my favorite song on the album."

6

MONSTER

When Gaga dedicated the song "Speechless" to her father at the Royal
Variety performance in England on December 7, 2009, he was in the audience
watching and admiring his little girl at work. Gaga and Joe had become closer as
her career took off. He had come through a serious bout of heart surgery—which
provided some of the inspiration for "Speechless"—and by the end of 2009 was
back at the center of his daughter's life. Joe had helped Gaga set up companies that
would administrate her publishing, touring, merchandizing, and Haus activities, and
they were all run out of Apt 1A at 135 W 70th Street, NY.

Registered in July 2008 at the Germanotta home were Haus of Gaga Publishing and
Mermaid Touring Inc. They joined Joe Germanotta's company Guestwifi in the office
room of the family condo. Naturally Joe had registered the internet address ladygaga.
com as far back as 2006 via the Mermaid Music company he'd started in order to
manage Stefani's songs. Although Gaga had an L.A. residence, she didn't spend too
much time there and had told *New York Magazine* early in 2009, "I don't like Los
Angeles, the people are awful and terribly shallow, and everybody wants to be famous
but nobody wants to play the game."

In her first year as an L.A. resident Gaga had rewritten the rules of that game. No
longer was it enough simply to be famous; from now on you had to be monster
famous. Not only that, but to be truly monster famous as defined by Lady Gaga
you had to have a very special, almost intimate relationship with your fans. By using
Twitter wherever she was in the world, Gaga could and did keep in constant, personal
touch with her fans whom she called her "little monsters." Other stars may have
employed people to tweet for them, but not Gaga. She was the only person at the
end of @ladygaga and her fans all knew that.

MONSTER BALL ROLLING

ALMOST as soon as the Fame Ball Tour had ended in September 2009, Gaga was announcing another tour, for later in the year. The Fame Kills Tour was to be a shared headline affair, with rapper Kanye West. Like Gaga, but in a different way, he'd made a memorable appearance at the 2009 MTV Awards show. Unlike Gaga's performance though, Kanye's was unexpected and unrehearsed. When he leapt on stage to deride winner of the "Best Female Video" award Taylor Swift, and claim that (soon to be Gaga collaborator) Beyoncé Knowles should have won, he truly shocked the audience who booed him off the stage.

In the weeks following the awards show, in attempting to apologize and win back favor lost by his actions, Kanye had quoted the fact that he'd not had any time away from work since the death of his mother in late 2007. Quite how another tour, albeit such a genre-busting one as Fame Kills was planned to be, would help his exhaustion was questionable. Gaga, who'd won the Best Newcomer Award for "Poker Face," tried to help West by agreeing to the tour and making public statements in his favor. However, making the strange statement that "Kanye and I are married" only further confused the media and fans more.

There wasn't much surprise then, when, despite dates being set out in September for an early November beginning for the Fame Kills Tour, on October 1 it was announced that the tour was cancelled. Instead, Gaga fans were to get another chance to see their idol in action, on a solo headline tour, titled The Monster Ball beginning on November 27 in Canada.

The use, once again, of the word "Ball" in the tour title reflects Gaga's growing relationship with her fans. People are invited to a Ball, rather than simply buying tickets for a gig. A Ball implies something more than a passive recreation, it suggests more of a shared experience and an event, with dancing and dressing up. A Ball has magical connotations (think *Cinderella* or *Beauty and the Beast*), romantic possibilities, and possible memories of prom nights past, or in anticipation of one to come. A Ball involves everyone present taking part in what makes the night special, not just the performers on stage. Gaga had wanted the Fame Kills Tour to use an enormous stage that ran across the floor of every venue like a fashion catwalk, allowing fans to be on every side of the action. That wasn't going to be physically possible, but still Gaga wanted to involve her little monsters as much as possible every night she performed, she wanted them at the center of the night's action and performance.

In describing what the Monster Ball would be like before it began Gaga said, "It is trash-sophisticated. I would say that it's futuristic, but still classic. I take a lot of my references from the '70s, and from European fashion mostly because they're ahead of us. I try to stay in tune with what's going on over there. So, my style is fashion-forward." The flyers and tickets for the first leg of the tour at the end of 2009 showed Gaga wearing "the orbit" outfit first seen on NBC's *Saturday Night Live* in October, and consists of a revolving sculpture that makes it seem as if Gaga is floating within it as she walks (wearing impossibly high heels, bikini bottoms, and shiny top). Designed by young British milliner Nasir Mazhar with the Haus of Gaga, it is certainly futuristic.

The show itself was to evolve as it progressed, with bits of film (again employed to give Gaga time for costume changes) added and subtracted, some of which were contributed by fans who'd shot footage from the crowd. There were also songs added to the setlist as they developed, making it more of the "pop-electro-opera" she wanted it to be.

Opposite: Just one of the spectacular sets used on the Monster Ball Tour, shown here at Radio City Music Hall, New York, on January 20, 2010.

"The whole point of what I do—The Monster Ball, the music, the performance aspect of it—I want to create a space for my fans where they can feel free and they can celebrate."

BAD ROMANCE

GAGA's appearance on *Saturday Night Live* in October 2009 wearing the orbit outfit was to perform a medley of songs that included part of "Bad Romance," the first single to be taken from the *Fame Monster* album. The song's first full public airing, however, came on October 7 at Alexander McQueen's Plato Atlantis catwalk show during Paris fashion week. It blasted out as models showed off his amazing creations while walking in those now famous lobster-claw shoes.

That first performance with Gaga alone on stage at a piano on *SNL* was important not only because it included some of "Bad Romance." It reminded everybody of Gaga's great musical ability and vocal strength, too. It was a throwback to her days even before she had become Gaga in some ways and proved that her songs were instant pop classics that can be played by anyone with musical ability.

Gaga's next two TV performances, on *The Jay Leno Show* and (for her fourth time in a year) *The Ellen DeGeneres Show*, both showcased "Bad Romance." The *Jay Leno* performance began with her singing a cappella before the band and backing tape kicked in, while on *Ellen* she

began at a piano before the band joined in with her. Along with a performance filmed for the *Gossip Girl* series, titled "The Last Days of Disco Stick," and a live performance on the American Music Awards, the TV appearances helped put the single at Number 14 on the *Billboard Hot 100* on its release—the highest debut for Gaga. The song became not only her fifth consecutive Number 1 hit on *Billboard*'s Pop Songs chart, but also became the most played single on radio in that chart's history. It also hit Number 1 on *Billboard*'s Digital Download Chart and went on to sell more than three million downloads in America.

The video for the single, directed by music video specialist Francis Lawrence, was another mini-movie. In it Gaga is made to dress up and perform for wealthy gangster-types who bid for her, as if she's a futuristic slave girl. Despite the lyrics implying that Gaga wants the "bad romance" that she and the person she's singing to seem to enjoy, the video ends with Gaga immolating the winning bidder for her sexual services. The final shot is of an ash-grimed Gaga with cigarette in mouth and her fire-breathing brassiere spouting sparks as she lies on a burned bed next to a charred skeleton.

The outfits worn in the video make it a fabulous fashion parade, but it's also a strong feminist statement—one picked up by the *L.A. Times* and remarked on in their interview with Gaga in December 2009. Addressing the writer Ann Powers, Gaga said, "I'm getting the sense that you're a little bit of a feminist, like I am, which is good." Powers goes on to state that, "Gaga's casual use of the term 'feminist' was interesting; like many female pop stars, she's rejected the term in the past. But she's evolving." Which is exactly what Gaga had been saying.

Her next video would show Gaga evolving once more, with yet more wit and invention.

Previous page: On stage, in a glass and metal box with a piano on fire. Gaga does the American Music Awards her way, Los Angeles, November 2009.

Opposite: Poster for the Monster Ball Tour. These particular performances were in Vancouver, Canada, December 2009.

"*The video for 'Bad Romance' is about . . . how the entertainment industry can, in a metaphorical way, simulate human trafficking—products being sold, the woman perceived as a commodity.*"

LADY | GAGA
THE MONSTER BALL
December 9 & 10
Queen Elizabeth Theatre

LADY GAGA
THE FAME MONSTER

BUY TICKETS AT LIVENATION.com

LADYGAGA.COM
MYSPACE.COM/LADYGAGA

IN STORES
November 24

NO TIME
FOR LOVE

A YEAR on from telling *New York Magazine*, "I'm from New York. I will kill to get what I want," Gaga pretty much had what she wanted and hadn't killed anyone—although men, whether boyfriends or the highest bidder, did seem to suffer grisly ends in her videos. The character of a boyfriend in the video of "Paparazzi" may or may not have been a representation of her first true love, bar manager Luc Carl who dumped her in 2008. When Carl had dared to tell Gaga that he didn't think that she would ever make it, she'd responded by telling him that one day he wouldn't be able to go into a deli without hearing her voice. What consolation she took from being right about that might have offset the fact that she'd sacrificed any kind of private romantic life in order to get onto every radio station's playlist.

It wasn't just the fact that Gaga had worked non-stop from the moment she arrived in L.A. that made it impossible to enjoy a "private" life; there was also the constant watching, the attention she received from strangers with cameras or online bloggers who seemed obsessed with discovering who she was sleeping with. For a while Gaga allowed rumors to circulate that she was "with" a dubious character known only as Speedy. The mythical media constructs known as "sources close to" and "close friends of" Gaga were "quoted" as reporting that Gaga and Speedy were in an on-off relationship. Remarkably, there were no photographs of Speedy taken and he gave no interviews to anyone about his love affair with the planet's most famous woman, even after their relationship was quoted as being very definitely "off." Either Speedy is the world's last great old-fashioned gentleman who refuses to kiss and tell, or he never existed.

There were also persistent internet-fuelled rumors that Gaga is gay. As is her way, the Lady does mischievous things, which encourage the lunatic fringe into believing any fantastic idea

that arises. Kissing women in her videos only added to the constant chatter about Gaga. That's how she wants it, especially when she's trying to reach as many people as possible via her records and shows. But . . .

The stresses of touring haven't changed since the days of steam trains and traveling carnivals. In numerous online and via-telephone interviews, Gaga has been reported as having to ask someone with her what town she's in as she speaks. The uniformity of hotels, the constant traveling, and performing on the same stage set every night all add to the disorientating effect of being constantly somewhere new every day. At least she surrounded herself while on the road with Haus members who she'd known for a while and feels she can trust. Matty "Dada" Williams, the creative director of the Haus, has been described as a former boyfriend. He, along with choreographer Laurie Ann Gibson (L.A.G.) remained close to and worked with Gaga as the Monster Ball rolled out around the world.

So too did at least three dancers who'd first hooked up with Gaga in 2008: Michael Silas (a.k.a. Mikey Mugler, Mickey McGlaire), Ian McKenzie (a.k.a. Louis Lagerfield), and Asiel Hardison (a.k.a. Duke Jones). Gaga's manager, Troy Carter, had become another constant in her life along with Vince Herbert and Martin Kierszenbaum. When she's in New York, of course, she has the family to look after her.

"I am a free-spirited woman: I have had boyfriends, and I have hooked up with women, but it's never been like 'I discovered gayness when I was dot dot dot.'"

GAGA GOD
RAINER MARIA RILKE

"Confess to yourself in the deepest hour of the night whether you would have to die if you were forbidden to write. Dig deep into your heart, where the answer spreads its roots in your being, and ask yourself solemnly, 'Must I write?'"

Gaga's interpretation of her Rilke tattoo

LETTER TO A YOUNG POET

Of all Lady Gaga's tattoos, the most surprising is perhaps the one written in German along the inside of her left arm. The CND logo, the heart with "dad" inside, the flowers to cover the treble clef are exactly the kind of cute, everyday body ornamentation that you'd expect to find on a young female pop star of the early twenty-first century. But a quote in the original German from a long-dead Austrian poet philosopher? That is seriously interesting.

Originally christened René, Rainer Maria Rilke was born in Prague (then capital of Bohemia) in 1875, and died of leukemia in Switzerland in 1926. A sensitive child, Rilke didn't finish school and learned everything from his own reading. In his early twenties he fell in love with a much older married woman (Lou Andreas-Salomé) who studied to be a psychoanalyst under Freud, and he enjoyed her company for three years. However, at the age of twenty-six Rilke became involved with the Modernist art movement and met German sculptress Clara Westhoff, whom he married in 1901. After only a year of living together (during which they had a daughter) Rilke moved to Paris alone, to work with sculptor Rodin. That move helped turn Rilke into an original, rather than classically inclined, poet.

Rodin encouraged Rilke to write from his heart, to put real feelings—fears as well as hopes—into his work. The sculptor helped Rilke to become a true artist. At the time of Rilke's move to Paris, he was in written communication with a nineteen-year-old Austrian military student in Austria named Franz Krappus, who had approached Rilke asking for criticism of his poetry. Between 1903 and 1908 Rilke wrote ten letters to Krappus, none of which offered literary criticism, all of which offered thoughts and opinions on life and how to live it. The quote Gaga has tattooed on her arm is taken from the very first letter written by Rilke to Krappus on February 17, 1903.

The German text in the original letter reads: "Prüfen Sie, ob er in der tiefsten Stelle Ihres Herzens seine Wurzeln ausstreckt, gestehen Sie sich ein, ob Sie sterben müßten, wenn es Ihnen versagt würde zu schreiben. Dieses vor allem: fragen Sie sich in der stillsten Stunde Ihrer Nacht: *muß* ich schreiben?" The translation most commonly given is "Confess to yourself whether you would have to die if you were forbidden to write. This most of all: ask yourself in the most silent hour of your night: 'Must I write?'" This version is taken from the English translation by Stephen Mitchell (Vintage, 1986).

Rilke's letters have been a source of inspiration for countless poets and artists since their first publication in 1929. The most prominent New York musician to quote Rilke is probably New Wave punk poet Patti Smith (a former lover of fashion and art photographer Robert Mapplethorpe and fringe Warhol Factory artist in the 1970s). But there are many others.

The last years of Rilke's life were dedicated to following his artistic ideals and pursuing his goals in spite of any criticism—he told Krappus in the first letter not to ever read criticism. That, as much as the beauty and poetry of his work, is doubtless what appeals to Lady Gaga.

Previous page: Performing in Francesco Vezzoli's "Ballets Russes Italian Style" during the Museum of Contemporary Art anniversary gala in Los Angeles, November 2009.

Opposite (top): Gaga discusses her new tattoo during the German TV show "Wetten, dass . . .?" (You Bet) in November 2009.

Opposite (bottom left): The man himself: Rilke.

ENDORSE ME

As well as promoting both the *Monster* album and Monster Ball Tour, Gaga had a totally different product to sell to her fans. "Heartbeats by Lady Gaga" in-ear headphones were first seen in October 2009. Their name and that of the company who makes them is one of those perfect and happy coincidences that occur all too rarely. Monster Cable Products had been founded in 1979 by an ex-drummer named Noel Lee, who was determined to produce great audio cable for the business and consumer. They are of course generally known as just "Monster."

Gaga was introduced to Monster Cable by record boss Jimmy Iovine. He and Interscope artist Dr. Dre had forged a working relationship with Monster to design iPod earphones that produced the kind of sound that Dre wanted to hear, and with the added bonus that the cable didn't get tangled up in your pockets. Monster had developed and patented a unique flat, ribbon-like cable that worked perfectly on both counts. Their first product together, a set of

$350 'phones called "Beats by Dr. Dre" went on sale in July 2008 after two years of development. The launch was so successful that in August 2008 Monster and Dre launched a range of new headphones called Monster Beats and included a pair of $149 in-ear headphones (the Tour set).

Naturally the name of the company appealed to Gaga, as did the chance to be associated with such a cool product, which she got to design herself (with help from design consultancy Ammunition). Unlike the discreet, red and black in-ear Tour set by Dre, Gaga's "Heartbeats" come in bright colors—bright chrome, black chrome, or rose red—and can be worn as fashion accessories with function. The dimpled texture to the angular heart-shaped exterior of the headphones gives them a distinctly futuristic feel. The cable has a flat-brushed chrome plate housing the playback controls, bearing a hand-drawn heart and Lady Gaga signature. The Heartbeats, retailing at between $99 and $130, went on sale around the world as the Monster Ball began its trek across the globe.

Below: The promotional flyer for the Heartbeat earphones.

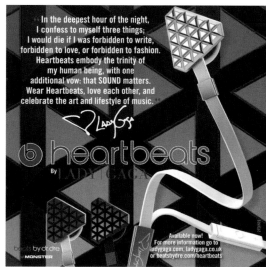

"I wore studded leather jackets, me and my friends in New York . . . Lifestyle, grit, passion, and love for music, freedom. These were the things I thought about when we were designing [the headphones]. So they really reflect a headphone that I just think is really great looking and represents who I am."

On January 7, 2010, Gaga made an appearance at the Consumer Electronics Show in Las Vegas, despite being scheduled that night to play in St. Louis. Talking at the Polaroid booth she told everyone how "exciting" it was to have been appointed creative director and inventor of novelty products for the brand. In a press release she was quoted as saying that, "The Haus of Gaga has been developing prototypes in the vein of fashion/technology/photography innovation—blending the iconic history of Polaroid and instant film with the digital era—and we are excited to collaborate on these ventures with the Polaroid brand." While at the convention Gaga also appeared with Dr. Dre to launch another set of Monster Beats headphones—the Red set—money from sales of which goes to AIDS-related charities. For Gaga the link to Polaroid brought her—yet again—closer to the legend of Andy Warhol, whose series of Polaroid portraits of famous people were both the basis for silkscreened artworks and considered works of art in themselves.

Being the headline star at the launch of both products in Vegas represented an enormous leap in her career from the previous year. In January 2009 she met Paris Hilton at the launch of a new cell phone in London. That night Paris was the headline star. From now on it could only be Gaga who got first billing.

Above: The new Polaroid creative director at the Consumer Electronics Show in Las Vegas, January 7, 2010.

"I'm living my dream right now. I'm on the road, I'm making music, I'm making art, I'm performing at arenas and in nightclubs and people know my lyrics, they know my fashion, and they know what I'm trying to say and it's affecting them. This is great. This is exactly what I've always wanted."

SPEECHLESS

THE appearance by Gaga in Vegas to promote her new role at Polaroid and the charity-benefitting Monster headphones, when she had a gig that night in St. Louis, was typical of the insane schedule she had been following for the past year. However much Gaga might have wanted to be everywhere, to do everything, and give time to everyone, it was just not physically possible. Yet, she'd seemingly been doing it all, non-stop, for so long that rumors began to circulate that there was more than one Gaga out there. Of course there was only one Gaga and she was, surprisingly perhaps, only human. In mid-January 2010 her body told her that she had to take a break or it would break on her.

Just two hours before she was scheduled to take the stage at Purdue University in West Lafayette, Indiana, on January 15, Gaga started feeling unwell. She was having difficulty breathing, heart palpitations, and was feeling dizzy. The Monster Ball support acts Jason Derullo and Semi Precious Weapons performed their sets while Gaga tried to find the strength to go on stage, but by 9:30 p.m. it was clear that she would be unable to perform that night. The news was as devastating for Gaga as it was for her audience. "I've been crying for hours," tweeted the singer later that night, "I feel like I let my fans down 2nite. I could hear my fans cheering from my dressing room, I begged everyone to let me go onstage. My stage has complicated mechanical elements, everyone was concerned I'd be in danger during the 2hr show, since I had passed out earlier. I am so devastated." She went on to reveal that she had previously performed while unwell—with the flu, a cold, strep throat—but that night she was feeling far more than discomfort.

Bewilderingly for Gaga's fans from Indiana, she appeared 'live' the next morning singing a medley and then being interviewed on the *Oprah Winfrey Friday Live* show. In the interview she said that she'd enjoyed chickens and waffles for breakfast and looked completely herself. There was no mention made of the previous night's collapse and cancelation. But then, perhaps because the show had been taped the previous weekend when Gaga played three nights at the Chicago Theatre (*Oprah Live* is recorded in Chicago), there wasn't likely to be. While *Oprah Live* sells itself as a live show, that definition is covered by the live performance made by each week's music act; they're not miming, they're playing "live."

Gaga's exhaustion was not being faked. She had to cancel the proposed next three concerts, one in Atlantic City and two in Connecticut. If she hoped to continue with the tour—and there were five dates at New York's prestigious Radio City Hall booked for the Monster Ball planned for January 20 through 24 to be played before the re-scheduled Purdue date on Jan 26—then she had to take it easy. At least she'd have three weeks between the Purdue performance and the next Ball, which was planned for Manchester in the UK.

Plus, before heading to Europe, Gaga had to make the video for her next single release, which was to be "Telephone." The song and the video both feature Beyoncé in a big, and surprising, way, and the filming was to be done on January 28 outside Los Angeles. Three days later Gaga had an appointment with the cameras at the 52nd Annual Grammy Awards at the Staples Center in L.A. There'd be time after that for Gaga to get her body back in shape for the next long and exotic leg of the Monster Ball Tour.

Previous page: Gaga at the Mac Viva Glam launch in London, March 2010. Cosmetic brand Mac has a range of products under the Viva Glam Gaga badge, sales of which support the MAC AIDS Fund.

Opposite: Making an entrance at the Grammy Awards, Los Angeles, January 2010.

"Me and my friends are in New York and we are going to The Monster Ball, but we get lost. Our car breaks down and we are having trouble getting there. I tell everyone, 'When you come to the Monster Ball it will set you free and all of the things that you don't like about yourself won't matter anymore.'"

MY LITTLE MONSTERS

When the Monster Ball began to roll again in Europe in late February 2010, it demonstrated an evolution from the first leg. Before the opening in November Gaga had spoken about how extravagant she wanted the show to be, and also how members of her Haus team had been trying to restrict some of the more spectacular ideas she'd had. They were—as always, she implied—to lose the battle, although it was to prove impossible to put some of the big ideas into the show for the smaller venues on the first leg of the tour. That was because of the time she had to put it together—the tour was booked in October and began in November. But since Gaga had said that the Monster Ball was about evolution, so the show itself evolved as it progressed. The second leg of the tour, all of which took place in arenas, was larger and more expensive than the first leg.

As the first leg came to an end Gaga told MTV, "for the next version of the Monster Ball, which is going to be in February when I begin in the UK with my arena tour, I'm throwing out the stage. My team thinks I'm completely psychotic. But I don't care what they think." Of course she cared what the Haus thought, it was just that Gaga doesn't like to hear "no" when she asks for something to be done. Especially when it concerned how her fans, those ever-precious little monsters, were to see her and be entertained by her.

During an appearance on the *Oprah* show Gaga seemed to choke up when talking about the "love" she had for her fans and how she felt for them. Everything she did was for them, she's reiterated time and again. The near-tears seemed to suggest that she was close to a mini-breakdown on TV, but the moment when she might have lost it completely passed.

Not even the announcement that all the ticket money for her Radio City show on January 24, and that all merchandising sales made via ladygaga.com on the same day, would go to a Haiti relief fund (a massive earthquake had devastated the country on January 12) was as emotional as that moment when she looked directly at the dressed-up little monsters in Oprah's audience, and told them she loved them. The tales of exhaustion and emotional collapse from the tour appeared to be true at that point.

Where the first part of the Monster Ball Tour had featured a mixture of films and performance in a way similar to the Fame Ball—though the Monster Ball was longer—the second leg was structured more like a Broadway show. Broken into four "acts," each was separated by a film and began with an interlude, which was made up from footage shot during the first leg of the Monster Ball. The interludes, titled *Puke Film*, *The Tornado*, *Antler Film*, and *Raven Film*, also included specially recorded a capella versions of Gaga numbers sung by the Lady. The *Monster Film* featured Gaga reciting a slightly longer version of the Manifesto of Little Monsters over black-and-white images.

The Act structure of Monster Ball part 2 followed a storyline of Gaga and her friends (the dancers) making their way to the Monster Ball. They began with the broken down car in the city (Act I), and the section included a new song "Glitter and Grease," plus the little-heard "Vanity" (only sold as a download at one site in 2008). The gang then entered the subway (Act II) for seven songs (plus the *Tornado* interlude film), the last of which was "So Happy I Could Die." They emerged into a forest (Act III) for four numbers and the Little Monster *Manifesto* film, the act ending with "Poker Face." Gaga and gang finally arrived at the Monster Ball (Act IV) and after battling the paparazzi during "Paparazzi," the final number ("Bad Romance") is performed with Gaga wearing her orbit dress.

During each show Gaga performed nineteen songs (sometimes more) and went through half a dozen or more costume changes as the set changed, films ran, and her little monsters filmed every moment on their cell phones.

Opposite: The Monster Ball Tour, 2010.
Top: Performing in Manchester, England, February 18. Bottom: Onstage in London, February 26.

"I hope you can forgive me. I love my little monsters more than anything, you are everything to me."

"I spend my money on my shows and on disappearing. I hate the paparazzi but the truth is, you can control it. If you put as much money into your security as you put into your diamonds or your jewelry, you can just disappear. People who say that they can't get away are lying. They must like the big flashes."

JOANNE

A T the end of Gaga's Manifesto for Little Monsters (on the *Fame Monster* CD sleeve) the date of 12/18/1974 is written. Gaga repeats the date in the Monster Ball interlude film, *Monster*, played during Act III of the Ball, which contains a longer version of the manifesto read by Gaga as images of her and others appear in black and white, all wearing leather studded fetish masks and monster hoods. The date is of the day that her aunt Joanne died, at the age of nineteen, from lupus. On the *Oprah* show Gaga revealed that before going on stage each night she and her dancers all join together in a circle to pray and end their huddle by chanting Joanne's name (which is also Gaga's second given name). Just as David Bowie's *Aladdin Sane* album (see page 56) was dedicated to his deceased brother, and at the time of the album's release in 1973 the singer talked of channeling his sibling's spirit, so Gaga has talked of how she feels that she has two hearts at times and one of them belongs to her aunt. It also reminds Gaga every night of where she's from, whom she can trust, and where to go when she needs sustenance, advice, unconditional love, and the space to simply be who she is: back to Joe and Cynthia's apartment in New York. "I bought my parents a Rolls Royce," she revealed in May 2010. "I had it delivered on their wedding anniversary, with a huge bow on it and the message: 'A car to last like a love like yours.'"

There should be no questioning the connection Gaga feels to her fans, either. She has an understanding of what it feels like to be rejected, remember—all those failed auditions she went through while at CAP21 added to the feeling of frustration she suffered when, first as a solo performer, and then as singer with SGBand, she failed to get any kind of big following or a record contract. That must have felt an awful lot like failure. When she was trying to break into the business there were always people ready to say "no" to Stefani.

When Def Jam dumped her before she had

even a chance at recording anything for them, the experience was followed sharply by being told by the love of her life that he didn't think that she'd ever "make it." So Gaga has known rejection and disappointment and has had people telling her how to act, dress, look, and perform. But as Lady Gaga she has made herself into a unique, unconventional, and unwavering star. Her message to her fans is that it is more than OK to be who you are— it's essential! As she also said on the *Oprah* show before heading off to Europe and Asia for almost six months, it's important to love your parents and family.

When former songwriting partner and producer Rob Fusari filed a lawsuit against Gaga on March 20, 2010, it must have seemed like another person who used to be close was attacking her. Gaga countersued—what else could she do?—and the pair could be involved in a lengthy court battle, over what he claims are lost revenues owing to him, for years. Or they could settle out of court. Either way, Fusari's actions reminded Gaga that real family were the only people she could rely on.

"It's hard knowing who to trust with your personal life. When you cry in your room at night, you don't always know who to call. So I am very close to my family."

TELEPHONE

JUST as Gaga set off for Europe at the end of January 2010, the second single to be taken from the *Fame Monster* album was released to radio stations. "Telephone" had originally emerged from a songwriting collaboration Gaga had enjoyed with Rodney "Darkchild" Jerkins, a Grammy Award–winning producer and songwriter (he produced Beyoncé and Jay-Z's hit single "Déjà Vu"). They worked together on songs intended for the Pussycat Dolls, but when "Telephone" didn't make it onto the *Doll Domination* album it was sent to Britney—who didn't include it on her *Circus* album, despite supposedly loving it. Britney's loss was Gaga's gain. "When Rodney and I were done [writing 'Telephone']", explained Gaga, "I was like, 'Oh my God, I want to sing it!' But my album was already closed." So it didn't make it onto *The Fame*. But when the song didn't make it onto Britney's *Circus* either, it left Gaga free to record a special version featuring vocalist Beyoncé Knowles and to include it on her sophomore album release.

The download track from *The Fame Monster* turned "Telephone" into a hit before the physical version of the single containing eleven remixes was released on March 2. In late November of 2009 Gaga had recorded a guest vocal on the eighth single to be taken from Beyoncé's *I Am . . . Sasha Fierce* album, titled "Video Phone." While that didn't become a big hit, making only Number 65 on the *Billboard Hot 100* chart, the experience of working together made both singers eager to do more. "Telephone" had proven to be a popular song with critics of *The Fame Monster*, and so before leaving America, Gaga and Beyoncé spent a day together making what would prove to be the year's most talked-about video—even with nine months of the year left to go.

When Gaga tweeted a tetchy message to people to ask them to stop "leaking" her video for "Telephone" in early March, it was clear that something special was in the can. When the video was finally unveiled on March 12, 2010, fans got to see another Jonas Akerlund mini-movie, albeit one a lot more unique than even "Paparazzi" had been. Gaga and Akerlund created a story which uses *Thelma and Louise* as its main influence, but brings in a range of other movie references, too. The use of the Pussy Wagon custom car from *Kill Bill*—loaned to Gaga by director Quentin Tarantino after they had a very Hollywood lunch together—is the most obvious.

There's also a nod to *Desperately Seeking Susan* in the hair, jacket, and makeup worn by Gaga in a jail scene that includes close-ups of her sister Natali. Then there are the "Wonder Woman"–style outfits worn by both singers in another scene.

In among the fake products shown off by Gaga and Beyoncé in the video, both of whom are made up to look like Helmut Newton–style models-as-mannequins, there are a bunch of genuine products. The clearest view is of a Virgin Mobile Services cell phone, but there are also Heartbeats headphones, the Dre Beats logo (on a prison guard's laptop computer), and Coke cans in Gaga's hair. The original Haus of Gaga products are the most interesting, of course. As well as the enormous chain dress

"There's certainly always a hidden message in my music videos, but I would say I'm mostly always trying to convolute everyone's idea of what a pop music video should be."

and sunglasses made of cigarettes, there are two fabulous telephone hats worn by Gaga.

However, a lingering lesbian kiss that Gaga enjoys with a masculine-looking "inmate" during an early scene prompted a lot of online and tabloid media chatter about the video.

Was Gaga saying that she—and by association, Beyoncé—are lesbians, asked the easily impressed with access to online forums? What does it matter, replies anyone with any sense: the world was talking about and watching the "Telephone" video.

Above: A relaxed Gaga wears the telephone hat by Philip Treacy on the *Friday Night with Jonathan Ross* TV show, London, March 2010.

FUTURE
LOVE

LADY Gaga began 2010 by picking up a lot of awards: There were two Grammys, one each for "Poker Face" and *The Fame*; three BRITs (one for "Poker Face," two for Gaga herself); a Meteor Award for Best International Female; an NRJ Music Award for "International Revelation"; two People's Choice Awards; and two NME Awards—one for Best Dressed, the other for Worst Dressed (readers get to vote). There were a lot of awards still pending at time of writing, and she'll undoubtedly be nominated for, and win, many more.

With certified album sales of *The Fame* and *The Fame Monster* in excess of ten million copies worldwide and six consecutive hit singles ("Telephone" made Number 3 on the *Hot 100* and Number 1 in the Pop Songs chart) and after two years of solid promotion, Gaga was a bona fide singing superstar everywhere in the world. "Alejandro," the third single to be taken from *The Fame Monster*, made it seven straight hit singles. Meanwhile album number three nears completion and certain success.

The only thing that could possibly stop Gaga from being the long-lasting star she wants to be is the fact that she is only human. Her ideas, vision, performance, and talent are all immense; her physical frame isn't. She's only a bit over five-feet tall and of slender build. The physical toil caused by her touring schedule resulted in a few missed performances, plus a couple of close calls early in 2010—she "collapsed" on stage in New Zealand in mid-March—but she won't be taking a break until all her dates are done ("I'd rather die on stage, with all my props, in front of my fans," she said in May 2010). Whatever else Gaga does with her body, she won't be indulging in casual sex, it seems. Speaking in London early in 2010, she said, "I can't believe I'm saying this—don't have sex. I'm single right now and I've chosen to be single because I don't have the time to get to know anybody. So it's OK not to have sex, it's OK to get to know people. I'm celibate, celibacy's fine." Speaking at the MAC VIVA AIDS awareness event (she's also launched a range of Gaga condoms), Gaga went on to let all her little monsters, especially those in their teens, know how they should just say "no" to sex if they're not ready for it. "I remember the cool girls when I was growing up," she said. "Everyone started to have sex. But it's not really cool anymore to have sex all the time." Her final sentence could easily be the Gaga manifesto in miniature: "It's cooler to be strong and independent."

Just as she did with *Monster*, Gaga wrote and recorded new songs while touring the Monster Ball, and those songs will make up her third album, which is loosely scheduled for release about the same time that this book is published. As she has said about herself, Gaga evolves very quickly and no matter who you are, by the time you think you've got her defined and think that you *know* Gaga, she's moved on.

This book has been constructed in order to help people in the future get an idea of how the Gaga phenomenon—for that's what she is—came into being and evolved. It can only act as a part-way marker in what promises to be a spectacular career. Enjoy the rest.

Opposite: Wowing the venerable Glastonbury Festival in England, June 2009.

"Ultimately you have to give up everything for your craft. If you are really serious about making music and being an artist as a full-time career, I would give up absolutely everything else and just go for it. I don't have relationships, I don't party any more. I spend every breathing moment making music and designing for the show and holding rehearsals. It's psychotic."

PICTURE CREDITS

The author and publishers have made every reasonable effort to contact all copyright holders. Any errors that may have occurred are inadvertent and anyone who for any reason has not been contacted is invited to write to the publishers so that a full acknowledgement may be made in subsequent editions of this work.

Page 2 Joe Furniss/WireImage; page 6 Ella Pellegrini/Newspix/Rex Features; page 8 Richard Ellis/Getty Images; page 10 John Grainger/Newspix/ Rex Features; page 12 Angus Smythe; pages 13–14 Seth Poppel/Yearbook Library; page 15 Angus Smythe; page 17 Sipa Press/Rex Features; page 18 Seth Poppel/Yearbook Library; page 19 Chris Polk/FilmMagic; page 20 Ken McKay/ITV/Rex Features; page 22 Chad Batka/Corbis; page 25 Sipa Press/Rex Features; page 26 Jemal Countess/Getty Images; page 28 Seth Poppel/Yearbook Library; page 29 Angus Smythe; page 30 Angela Wieland; page 32 (top) Tommy Cole; (bottom) Jim Linwood/Flickr; page 34 Theo Wargo/WireImage; page 37 Angela Wieland; page 38 WWD/ Condé Nast/Corbis; page 40 Tommy Cole; page 41 Angela Wieland; page 42 Simone Cecchetti/Corbis; page 44 Scott McLane/Retna Ltd./Corbis; page 47 (top) John Parra/WireImage; (bottom) Bettmann/Corbis; page 48 Angus Smythe; page 49 Veronica Ibarra; page 50 Angela Wieland; page 52 Veronica Ibarra; page 53 Veronica Ibarra; page 54 Jason Squires/WireImage; page 57 Mark Allan/WireImage; page 58 Scott Gries/Getty Images; page 60 Tommy Cole; page 62 Kevin Mazur/WireImage; page 63 Robert Knight Archive/Redferns; page 64 Veronica Ibarra; page 65 Amy Sussman/ Stringer/Getty Images; page 67 Cifra Manuela/Newspix/Rex Features; page 68 Jeff Kravitz/FilmMagic; page 70 Stephen Lovekin/Getty Images; page 72 Kevin Mazur/WireImage; page 73 Dimitrios Kambouris/Getty Images; page 74 POOL/Reuters/Corbis; page 75 Ilpo Musto/Rex Features; page 76 Theo Wargo/WireImage; page 79 (top) Kevork Djansezian/Getty Images; (bottom) Chad Batka/Corbis; page 81 Chelsea Lauren/WireImage; page 82 Larry Busacca/Getty Images; page 83 Sheila Rock/Rex Features; page 84 Yoshikazu Tsuno/AFP/Getty Images; page 85 Dennis Van Tine/ Retna Ltd./Corbis; Larry Busacca/Getty Images; pages 86–87 & page 88 (top) courtesy of V Magazine; page 88 (bottom) courtesy of Elle/Hachette Filipacchi Media; page 89 courtesy of Max/RCS Periodici; page 90 Sonia Moskowitz/Globe Photos; page 93 Brian Ach/Stringer/WireImage; page 94 Seth Browarnik/Rex Features; page 96 Don Arnold/WireImage; page 98 Darrin Zammit Lupi/Reuters/Corbis; page 100 Ronald Wittek/dpa/ Corbis; page 103 Brian Rasic/Rex Features; page 104 Mark Von Holden/Stringer/WireImage; page 106 Stefan M. Prager/Redferns; page 108 Mario Anzuoni/Reuters/Corbis; page 110 (top) Philippe Wojazer/Reuters/Corbis; (bottom) David Fisher/Rex Features; pages 113–114 George Pimentel/ WireImage; page 116 Kevin Mazur/WireImage; page 118 C. Flanigan/FilmMagic; page 119 Jeff Kravitz/FilmMagic; page 120 Matt Baron/BEI/ Rex Features; page 122 Michael Caulfield/Getty Images Entertainment; page 124 Mario Anzuoni/Reuters; page 127 Niki Nikolova/FilmMagic; page 128 PGR/Evan Agostini/Retna; page 130 Kevin Mazur/WireImage; page 132 Kevin Winter/AMA2009/Getty Images Entertainment; page 136 Kevin McKay/ITV/Rex Features; page 137 Kevin Mazur/WireImage; page 138 Mario Anzuoni/Reuters/Corbis; page 141 (top) POOL/Reuters/ Corbis; (bottom left) Imagno/Hulton Archive/Getty Images; (bottom right) Justin Campbell/BuzzFoto/FilmMagic; page 143 Mario Anzuoni/ Reuters/Corbis; page 144 Mike Marsland/WireImage; page 147 Christopher Polk/Getty Images; page 148 (top) Neil Lupin/Redferns; (bottom) Mark Campbell/Rex Features; page 150 Jakubaszek/Getty Images Entertainment; page 152 Larry Busacca/Getty Images Entertainment; page 155 Brian J. Ritchie/Hotsauce/Rex Features; page 157 Frantzesco Kangaris/Getty Images Entertainment; page 158–159 Fred Dofour/AFP/Getty Images.

SOURCES

Print

Los Angeles Times
The Guardian
The Times (London)
New York magazine
London Evening Standard
The Scotsman
Rolling Stone magazine
Elle magazine
Cosmopolitan magazine
Girl magazine
Mizz magazine
Interview magazine
Out magazine
Q magazine
Reuters
iProng magazine
New Musical Express
Chicago Tribune

Online

Hardcandymusic.com
About.com
   http://dancemusic.about.com/od/artistshomepages/a/LadyGagaInt.htm
starpulse.com
   http://www.starpulse.com/news/index.php/2008/10/24/interview_lady_gaga_chats_about_her_music
killahbeez.com
   http://www.killahbeez.com/2008/12/02/killahbeez-interview-with-lady-gaga/
blogcritics.org
   http://blogcritics.org/music/article/interview-lady-gaga-singer-and-songwriter/
artistdirect.com
   http://www.artistdirect.com/nad/news/article/0,,4931544,00.html
allthingsfangirl.blogspot.com
   http://allthingsfangirl.blogspot.com/2009/11/before-there-was-gaga-muse-da7e-sarah.html
webofdeception.com
   http://www.webofdeception.com/ladygaga.html
ladygaga.com
ladygaga.com.au
ladygaga.co.uk
perezhilton.com
ladygaga.wikia.com/wiki/Gagapedia
gagadaily.com
lady-gaga.net
ladygagaonline.com
lady-gaga.us